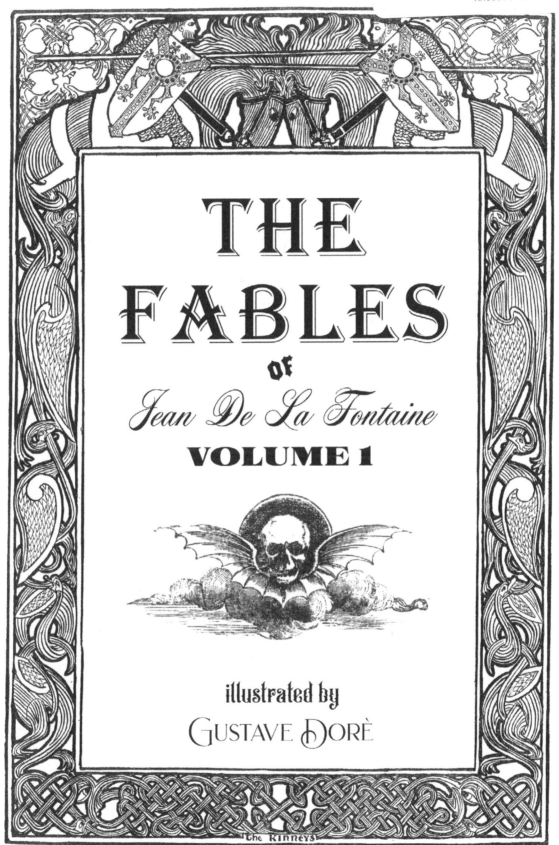

THE FABLES

OF

Jean De La Fontaine

VOLUME 1

illustrated by
GUSTAVE DORÈ

**The Fables of Jean De La Fontaine
Volume 1:
Gustave Doré Restored Special Edition**

Written by Jean De La Fontaine
Illustrations by Gustave Doré
Translated by Walter Thornbury
Cover design by Mark Bussler

Copyright © 2021 Inecom, LLC.
All Rights Reserved

No parts of this book may be reproduced or broadcast in any way without written permission from Inecom, LLC.

www.CGRpublishing.com

* * * * *

Preface on Page 358

Table of Contents on Page 364

THE ART EDITION.

THE FABLES

—OF—

JEAN DE LA FONTAINE,

Translated into English Verse

—BY—

WALTER THORNBURY.

TO WHICH IS ADDED

AN ESSAY ON HIS LIFE AND WORKS,

ALSO,

The Life of Æsop, the Phrygian.

Profusely Illustrated

—BY—

GUSTAVE DORÉ.

THE GRASSHOPPER AND THE ANT.

FABLE I.

THE GRASSHOPPER AND THE ANT.

THE Grasshopper, so blithe and gay,
    Sang the summer time away.
Pinched and poor the spendthrift grew,
When the sour north-easter blew.
In her larder not a scrap,
Bread to taste, nor drink to lap.
To the Ant, her neighbor, she
Went to moan her penury,
Praying for a loan of wheat,
Just to make a loaf to eat,
Till the sunshine came again.
" All I say is fair and plain,
I will pay you every grain,
Principal and interest too,
Before harvest, I tell you,
On my honor—every pound,

Ere a single sheaf is bound."
The Ant's a very prudent friend,
Never much disposed to lend;
Virtues great and failings small,
This her failing least of all,
Quoth she, "How spent you the summer?"
"Night and day to each new comer
I sang gaily, by your leave;
Singing, singing, morn and eve."
"You sang? I see it at a glance.
Well, then, now's the time to dance."

FABLE II.

THE RAVEN AND THE FOX.

MASTER RAVEN, perched upon a tree,
    Held in his beak a savory piece of cheese;
Its pleasant odor borne upon the breeze,
Allured Sir Reynard, with his flattery.
"Ha! Master Raven, 'morrow to you, sir;
How black and glossy! now, upon my word,
I never—beautiful! I do aver.
If but your voice becomes your coat, no bird
More fit to be the Phœnix of our wood—
I hope, sir, I am understood?"
The Raven, flattered by the praise,
Opened his spacious beak to show his ways
Of singing: down the good cheese fell.
Quick the Fox snapped it. "My dear sir, 'tis well,"
He said. "Know that a flatterer lives
On him to whom his praise he gives;

And, my dear neighbor, an' you please,
This lesson's worth a slice of cheese.—
The Raven vexed at his consenting,
Flew off, too late in his repenting.

FABLE III.

THE FROG THAT WISHED TO MAKE HERSELF AS BIG AS THE OX.

A FROG, no bigger than a pullet's egg,
   A fat ox feeding in a meadow spied.
The envious little creature blew and swelled;
In vain to reach the big bull's bulk she tried.
"Sister, now look! observe me close!" she cried.
"Is this enough?"—"No!" "Tell me! now then, see!"
"No, no!" "Well, now I'm quite as big as he?"
"You're scarcely bigger than you were at first!"
One more tremendous puff—she grew so large—she burst.
The whole world swarms with people not more wise:
The tradesman's villa with the palace vies.
Ambassadors your poorest Princelings send,
And every Count has pages without end.

FABLE IV.

THE TWO MULES.

TWO Mules were journeying—one charged with oats,
  The other with a tax's golden fruit.
This last betrayed the manner which denotes
Excessive vanity in man or brute.
Proudly self-conscious of his precious load,
He paced, and loud his harness-bells resounded;
When suddenly upon their lonely road,
Both Mules and masters were by thieves surrounded.
The money-bearer soon was put to death:
"Is this the end that crowns my high career?
Yon drudge," he murmured with his latest breath,
"Escapes unhurt, while I must perish here!"
"My friend," his fellow-traveller made reply,
"Wealth cannot always at the poor man scoff.
If you had been content to do as I,
You'd not at present be so badly off."

THE TWO MULES.

FABLE V.

THE WOLF AND THE DOG.

A WOLF, who was but skin and bone,
So watchful, had the sheep-dogs grown,
Once met a Mastiff fat and sleek,
Stern only to the poor and weak.
Sir Wolf would fain, no doubt, have munched
This pampered cur, and on him lunched;
But then the meal involved a fight,
And he was craven, save at night;
For such a dog could guard his throat
As well as any dog of note.
So the Wolf, humbly flattering him,
Praised the soft plumpness of each limb.
" You're wrong, you're wrong, my noble sir,
To roam in woods indeed you err,"
The dog replies, " you do indeed;
If you but wish, with me you'll feed.

LA FONTAINE'S FABLES.

Your comrades are a shabby pack,
Gaunt, bony, lean in side and back,
Pining for hunger, scurvy, hollow,
Fighting for every scrap they swallow.
Come share my lot, and take your ease."
" What must I do to earn it, please ? "
" Do !—why, do nothing !   Beggar-men
Bark at and chase ; fawn now and then
At friends ; your master always flatter.
Do this, and by this little matter
Earn every sort of dainty dish—
Fowl-bones or pigeons'—what you wish—
Aye better things ; and with these messes,
Fondlings, and ceaseless kind caresses."
The Wolf, delighted, as he hears
Is deeply moved—almost to tears ;
When all at once he sees a speck,
A gall upon the Mastiff's neck.
" What's that ? "—" Oh, nothing !"   " Nothing ? "—" No !
" A slight rub from the chain you know."
" The chain ! " replies the Wolf, aghast ;
" You are not free ?—they tie you fast ? "
" Sometimes.   But, law ! what matters it ? "—
" Matters so much the rarest bit
Seems worthless bought at such a price."
The Wolf, so saying, in a trice,
Ran off and with the best goodwill,
And very likely's running still.

FABLE VI.

THE HEIFER, THE SHE-GOAT, AND THE LAMB, IN PARTNERSHIP WITH THE LION.

THE Heifer, Lamb, and Nanny-goat were neighbors,
   With a huge Lion living close at hand;
They shared the gains and losses of their labors,
   (All this was long ago, you understand).
One day a stag was taken as their sport;
   The Goat, who snared him, was of course enraptured,
And sent for all the partners of her toil
   In order to divide the treasure captured.
They came. The Lion, counting on his claws,
   Quartered the prey, and thus addressed the trio—
"The parts are four. I take the first, because
   I am your monarch, and my name is Leo:
Being the strongest, I annex the second;
   As bravest, I can claim another share;
Should any touch the fourth, or say I reckoned
   Unjustly, I shall kill him. So beware."

FABLE VII.

THE WALLET.

SAID Jupiter one day, " Let all that breathe
    Come and obeisance make before my throne.
If at his shape or being any grieve,
Let them cast fears aside.   I'll hear their groan.
Come, Monkey, you be first to speak.   You see
Of animals this goodly company;
Compare their beauties with your own.
Are you content?"   "Why not?   Good gracious me!"
      The monkey said,
      No whit afraid—
"Why not content?   I have four feet like others.
My portrait no one sneers at—do they, brothers?
But cousin Bruin's hurriedly sketched in,
And no one holds his likeness worth a pin."
Then came the Bear.   One thought he would have found
Something to grumble at.   Grumble! no, not he.

THE WALLET.

He praised his form and shape, but, looking round,
Turned critic on the want of symmetry
Of the huge shapeless Elephant, whose ears
Were much too long; his tail too short, he fears.
   The Elephant was next.
   Though wise, yet sadly vexed
To see good Madam Whale, to his surprise,
A cumbrous mountain of such hideous size.
Quick Mrs. Ant thinks the Gnat far too small,
Herself colossal.—Jove dismisses all,
Severe on others, with themselves content.
'Mong all the fools who that day homeward went,
Our race was far the worst: our wisest souls
Lynxes to others', to their own faults moles.
Pardon at home they give, to others grace deny,
And keep on neighbors' sins a sleepless eye.
   Jove made us so,
    As we all know,
We wear our Wallets in the self-same way—
This current year, as in the by-gone day:
In pouch behind our own defects we store,
The faults of others in the one before.

FABLE VIII.

THE SWALLOW AND THE LITTLE BIRDS.

A SWALLOW, in his travels o'er the earth,
    Into the law of storms had gained a peep;
Could prophesy them long before their birth,
    And warn in time the ploughmen of the deep.
Just as the month for sowing hemp came round,
    The swallow called the smaller birds together.
"Yon' hand," said he, "which strews along the ground
    That fatal grain, forebodes no friendly weather.
The day will come, and very soon, perhaps,
    When yonder crop will help in your undoing—
When, in the shape of snares and cruel traps,
    Will burst the tempest which to-day is brewing.
Be wise, and eat the hemp up now or never;
    Take my advice." But no, the little birds,
Who thought themselves, no doubt, immensely clever,
    Laughed loudly at the Swallow's warning words.

THE SWALLOW AND THE LITTLE BIRDS.

THE SWALLOW AND THE LITTLE BIRDS.

Soon after, when the hemp grew green and tall,
    He begged the birds to tear it into tatters.
"Prophet of ill," they answered one and all,
    "Cease chattering about such paltry matters."
The hemp at length was ripe, and then the Swallow,
    Remarking that "ill weeds were never slow,"
Continued—"Though it's now too late to follow
    The good advice I gave you long ago,
You still may manage to preserve your lives
    By giving credit to the voice of reason.
Remain at home, I beg you, with your wives,
    And shun the perils of the coming season.
You cannot cross the desert or the seas,
    To settle down in distant habitations.
Make nests, then, in the walls, and there, at ease,
    Defy mankind and all its machinations."
They scorned his warnings, as in Troy of old
    Men scorned the lessons that Cassandra taught;
And shortly, as the Swallow had foretold,
    Great numbers of them in the traps were caught.

To instincts not our own we give no credit,
And till misfortune comes, we never dread it.

FABLE IX.

THE TOWN RAT AND THE COUNTRY RAT.

A RAT from town, a country Rat
    Invited in the civilest way;
For dinner there was just to be
    Ortolans and an entremet.

Upon a Turkey carpet soft
    The noble feast at last was spread;
I leave you pretty well to guess
    The merry, pleasant life they led.

Gay the repast, for plenty reigned,
    Nothing was wanting to the fare;
But hardly had it well begun
    Ere chance disturbed the friendly pair.

A sudden racket at the door
    Alarmed them, and they made retreat;
The City Rat was not the last,
    His comrade followed fast and fleet.

THE TOWN RAT AND THE COUNTRY RAT.

THE TOWN RAT AND THE COUNTRY RAT.

The noise was over, they returned,
    As rats on such occasions do;
"Come," said the liberal citizen,
    "And let us finish our ragout."

"Not a crumb more," the rustic said;
    "To-morrow you shall dine with me;
Don't think me jealous of your state,
    Or all your royal luxury;

"But then I eat so quiet at home,
    And nothing dangerous is near;
Good-bye, my friend, I have no love
    For pleasure when it's mixed with fear."

FABLE X.

THE MAN AND HIS IMAGE.
FOR M. THE DUKE DE LA ROCHEFOUCAULD.

A MAN who had no rivals in the love
   He bore himself, thought that he won the bell
From all the world, and hated every glass
That truths less palatable tried to tell.
Living contented in the error,
Of lying mirrors he'd a terror.
Officious Fate, determined on a cure,
Raised up, where'er he turned his eyes,
Those silent counsellors that ladies prize.
   Mirrors old and mirrors newer;
Mirrors in inns and mirrors in shops;
Mirrors in pockets of all the fops;
Mirrors in every lady's zone.
What could our poor Narcissus do?
He goes and hides him all alone

THE MAN AND HIS IMAGE.

In woods that one can scarce get through.
No more the lying mirrors come,
But past his new-found, savage home
A pure and limpid brook runs fair.—
He looks.   His ancient foe is there!
His angry eyes stare at the stream,
He tries to fancy it a dream.
Resolves to fly the odious place, and shun
The image; yet, so fair the brook, he cannot run.

    My meaning is not hard to see;
No one is from this failing free.
The man who loved himself is just the Soul,
The mirrors are the follies of all others.
(Mirrors are faithful painters on the whole;)
And you know well as I do, brothers, that the brook
Is the wise "Maxim-book."*

* Rochefoucauld's Maxims are the most extraordinary dissections of human selfishness ever made.

FABLE XI.

THE DRAGON WITH MANY HEADS, AND THE DRAGON WITH MANY TAILS.

AN Envoy of the Grand Signor
   (I can't say more)
One day, before the Emperor's court,
Vaunted, as some historians report,
That his royal master had a force
Outnumbering all the foot and horse
The Kaiser could bring to the war.
Then spoke a choleric attendant:
"*Our* Prince has more than *one* dependant
That keeps an army at his own expense."
The Pasha (man of sense),
Replied: "By rumor I'm aware
What troops the great electors spare
And that reminds me, I am glad,
Of an adventure I once had,

THE DRAGON WITH MANY HEADS, AND THE DRAGON WITH MANY TAILS.

"Strange and yet true.
I'll tell it you.

Once through a hedge the hundred heads I saw
Of a huge Hydra show.
My blood, turned ice, refused to flow:
And yet I felt that neither fang nor claw
Could more than scare me—for no head came near.
There was no room. I cast off fear.
While musing on this sight,
Another Dragon came to light.
Only one head this time,
But tails too many to count up in rhyme.
The fit again came on,
Worse than the one just gone.
The head creeps first, then follows tail by tail;
Nothing can stop their road nor yet assail;
One clears the way for all the minor powers:
The first's *your* Emperor's host, the second *ours*."

FABLE XII.

THE WOLF AND THE LAMB.

THE reasoning of the strongest has such weight
    None can gainsay it, or dare prate,
No more than one would question Fate.
A Lamb her thirst was very calmly slaking,
    At the pure current of a woodland rill;
A grisly Wolf, by hunger urged, came making
    A tour in search of living things to kill.
"How dare you spoil my drink?" he fiercely cried;
    There was grim fury in his very tone;
      "I'll teach you to let beasts like me alone."
"Let not your Majesty feel wrath," replied
The Lamb, "nor be unjust to me, from passion;
I cannot, Sire, disturb in any fashion
The stream which now your Royal Highness faces,
I'm lower down by at least twenty paces."
"You spoil it!" roared the Wolf; "and more, I know,

THE WOLF AND THE LAMB.

THE WOLF AND THE LAMB.

You slandered me but half a year ago."
"How could I do so when I scarce was born?"
The Lamb replied; "I was a suckling then."
"Then 'twas your brother held me up to scorn."
"I have no brother."   "Well, 'tis all the same;
At least 'twas some poor fool that bears your name.
You and your dogs, both great and small,
Your sheep and shepherds, one and all,
Slander me, if men say but true,
And I'll revenge myself on you."
Thus saying, he bore off the Lamb
Deep in the wood far from its dam,
And there, not waiting judge nor jury,
Fell to, and ate him in his fury.

FABLE XIII.

THE ROBBERS AND THE ASS.

TWO Thieves were fighting for a prize,
    A Donkey newly stolen; sell or not to sell—
That was the question—bloody fists, black eyes:
    While they fought gallantly and well,
        A third thief happening to pass,
        Rode gaily off upon the ass.

The ass is some poor province it may be;
    The thieves, that gracious potentate or this,
Austria, Turkey, or say Hungary;
Instead of two, I vow I've set down three
    (The world has almost had enough of this),
    And often neither will the province win:
    For third thief stepping in,
        'Mid their debate and noisy fray,
        With the disputed donkey rides away.

THE ROBBERS AND THE ASS.

FABLE XIV.

DEATH AND THE WOODCUTTER.

A POOR Woodcutter, covered with his load,
  Bent down with boughs, and with a weary age,
Groaning and stooping, made his sorrowing stage
To reach his smoky cabin; on the road,
Worn out with toil and pain, he seeks relief
By resting for a while, to brood on grief.—
What pleasure has he had since he was born?
In this round world is there one more forlorn?
Sometimes no bread, and never, never rest.
Creditors, soldiers, taxes, children, wife,
    The corvée.   Such a life!
The picture of a miserable man—look east or west.
He calls on Death—for Death calls everywhere—
    Well—Death is there.
    He comes without delay,
And asks the groaner if he needs his aid.

"Yes," said the Woodman, "help me in my trade.
Put up these faggots—then you need not stay."

Death is a cure for all, say I,
 But do not budge from where you are;
BETTER TO SUFFER THAN TO DIE,
 Is man's old motto, near and far.

DEATH AND THE WOODCUTTER.

FABLE XV.

SIMONIDES RESCUED BY THE GODS.

THREE sorts of persons can't be praised too much:
    The Gods, the King, and her on whom we doat.
So said Malherbe, and well he said, for such
    Are maxims wise, and worthy of all note.
Praise is beguiling, and disliked by none:
A lady's favor it has often won.
Let's see whate'en the gods have ere this done
    To those who praised them.   Once the eulogy
Of a rough athlete was in verse essayed.
Simonides, the ice well broken, made
    A plunge into a swamp of flattery.
The athlete's parents were poor folk unknown;
The man mere lump of muscle and of bone—
       No merit but his thews,
       A barren subject for the muse.
The poet praised his hero all he could,

LA FONTAINE'S FABLES.

Then threw him by, as others would.
    Castor and Pollux bringing on the stage,
He points out their example to such men,
    And to all strugglers in whatever age;
Enumerates the places where they fought,
And why they vanished from our mortal ken.
In fact, two-thirds of all his song was fraught
With praise of them, page after page.
A Talent had the athlete guaranteed,
But when he read he grudged the meed,
And gave a third: frank was his jest,—
" Castor and Pollux pay the rest;
Celestial pair! they'll see you righted,—
Still I will feast you with the best;
Sup with me, you will be delighted;
    The guests are all select, you'll see,
      My parents, and friends loved by me;
      Be thou, too, of the company."
Simonides consents, partly, perhaps in fear
    To lose, besides his due, the paltry praise.
He goes—they revel and discuss the cheer;
    A merry night prepares for jovial days.
A servant enters, tells him at the door
    Two men would see him and without delay.
He leaves the table, not a bit the more
    Do jaws and fingers cease their greedy play.
These two men were the Gemini he'd praised.
They thanked him for the homage he had paid;
Then, for reward, told him the while he stayed

SIMONIDES RESCUED BY THE GODS.

The doom'd house would be razed,
And fall about the ears
Of the big boxer and his peers.
The prophecy came true—yes, every tittle;
Snap goes a pillar, thin and brittle.
The roof comes toppling down and crashes
The feast—the cups, the flagons smashes.
Cupbearers are included in the fall;
    Nor is that all:
To make the vengeance for the bard complete,
The athlete's legs are broken too.
A beam snapped underneath his feet,
    While half the guests exclaim,
    "Lord help us! we are lame."
Fame, with her trumpet, heralds the affair;
Men cry, "A miracle!" and everywhere
They give twice over without scoff or sneer
To poet by the gods held dear.
No one of gentle birth but paid him well,
Of their ancestors' deeds to nobly tell.

Let me return unto my text: it pays
The gods and kings to freely praise;
Melpomene, moreover, sometimes traffic makes
Of the ingenious trouble that she takes.
Our art deserves respect, and thus
The great do honor to themselves who honor us.
    Olympus and Parnassus once, you see,
    Were friends, and liked each other's company.

FABLE XVI.

DEATH AND THE UNHAPPY MAN.

A MISERABLE Man incessant prayed
    To death for aid.
"Oh, Death!" he cried, "I love thee as a friend!
Come quickly, and my life's long sorrows end!"
Death, wishing to oblige him, ran,
Knocked at the door, entered, and eyed the man.
"What do I see? begone, thou hideous thing!
    The very sight
Strikes me with horror and affright!
Begone, old Death!—Away, thou grisly King!"
Mecænas (hearty fellow) somewhere said:
    "Let me be gouty, crippled, impotent and lame,
    'Tis all the same,
So I but keep on living. Death, thou slave!
Come not at all, and I shall be content."
And that was what the man I mention meant.

THE WOLF TURNED SHEPHERD.

FABLE XVII.

THE WOLF TURNED SHEPHERD.

A WOLF who found in cautious flocks
    His tithes beginning to be few,
Thought that he'd play the part of Fox,
    A character at least quite new.
A Shepherd's hat and coat he took,
And from a branch he made a hook;
Nor did the pastoral pipe forget.
To carry out his schemes he set,
He would have liked to write upon his hat,
    "I'm Guillot, Shepherd of these sheep!"

And thus disguised, he came, pit-pat,
    And softly stole where fast asleep
Guillot himself lay by a stack,
His dog close cuddling at his back;
His pipe too slept; and half the number
Of the plump sheep was wrapped in slumber.

He's got the dress—could be but mock
The Shepherd's voice, he'd lure the flock:
    He thought he could,
That spoiled the whole affair—he'd spoken;
    His howl re-echoed through the wood.
The game was up—the spell was broken!
    They all awake, dog, Shepherd, sheep.
      Poor Wolf, in this distress
      And pretty mess,
In clumsy coat bedight,
Could neither run away nor fight.

At last the bubble breaks;
There's always some mistake a rascal makes.
The Wolf like Wolf must always act;
That is a very certain fact.

FABLE XVIII.

THE CHILD AND THE SCHOOLMASTER

THIS fable serves to tell, or tries to show
    A fool's remonstrance often is in vain.
A child fell headlong in the river's flow,
    While playing on the green banks of the Seine:
A willow, by kind Providence, grew there,
The branches saved him (rather, God's good care);
Caught in the friendly boughs, he clutched and clung.
    The master of the school just then came by.
'Help! help! I'm drowning!" as he gulping hung,
    He shouts. The master, with a pompous eye,
Turns and reproves him with much gravity.
    "You little ape," he said, "now only see
What comes of all your precious foolery;
A pretty job such little rogues to guard.
Unlucky parents who must watch and thrash
Such helpless, hopeless, good-for-nothing trash.

I pity them; their woes I understand."
Having said this, he brought the child to land.

In this I blame more people than you guess—
    Babblers and censors, pedants, all the three;
Such creatures grow in numbers to excess,
    Some blessing seems to swell their progeny.
In every crisis theories they shape,
    And exercise their tongues with perfect skill;
Ha! my good friends, first save me from the scrape,
    Then make your long speech after, if you will.

FABLE XIX.

THE PULLET AND THE PEARL.

A FOWL, while scratching in the straw,
    Finding a pearl without a flaw,
      Gave it a lapidary of the day.
"It's very fine, I must repeat;
And yet a single grain of wheat
      Is very much more in my way."

A poor, uneducated lad
A manuscript as heirloom had.
      He took it to a bookseller one day.
"I know," said he, "it's very rare;
But still, a guinea as my share
      Is very much more in my way."

FABLE XX.

THE DRONES AND THE BEES.

A WORKMAN by his work you always know.
    Some cells of honey had been left unclaimed.
        The Drones were first to go
        The Bees to try and show
That they to take the mastership were not ashamed.
Before a Wasp the cause at last they bring;
It is not easy to decide the thing.
The witnesses deposed that round the hive
They long had seen wing'd, buzzing creatures fly,
Brown, and like bees. "Yes, true; but, man alive,
The Drones are also brown; so do not try
To prove it so." The Wasp, on justice bent,
        Made new investigations
           (Laws of all nations).
To throw more light upon the case,

THE DRONES AND THE BEES.

Searched every place,
Heard a whole ants' nest argue face to face,
Still it grew only darker; that's a fact,
   (Lease or contract?)
"Oh, goodness gracious! where's the use, my son?"
   Cried a wise Bee;
   "Why, only see,
For six months now the cause is dragging on,
And we're no further than we were at first;
 But what is worst,
  The honey's spoiling, and the hive is burst.
'Tis time the judge make haste,
The matter's simmered long enough to waste,
 Without rebutters or *fi*, *fa*,
 Without rejoinders or *ca*, *sa*,
   John Doe
   Or Richard Roe.
Let's go to work, the wasp and us,
 We'll see who best can build and store
The sweetest juice." It's settled thus.
 The Drones do badly, as they've done of yore;
The art's beyond their knowledge, quite beyond.
 The Wasp adjudges that the honey goes
Unto the Bees: would those of law so fond
 Could thus decide the cases justice tries.
Good common sense, instead of Coke and code,
 (The Turks in this are really very wise,)
Would save how many a debtor's heavy load.
  Law grinds our lives away
  With sorrow and delay.

In vain we groan, and grudge
    The money given to our long-gowned tutors.
Always at last the oyster's for the judge,
    The shells for the poor suitors.

THE OAK AND THE REED.

FABLE XXI.

THE OAK AND THE REED.

THE Oak said one day to a river Reed,
    "You have a right with Nature to fall out.
Even a wren for you's a weight indeed;
    The slightest breeze that wanders round about
        Makes you first bow, then bend;
While my proud forehead, like an Alp, braves all,
Whether the sunshine or the tempest fall—
A gale to you to me a zephyr is.
Come near my shelter: you'll escape from this;
    You'll suffer less, and everything will mend.
        I'll keep you warm
        From every storm;
And yet you foolish creatures needs must go,
And on the frontiers of old Boreas grow.
    Nature to you has been, I think, unjust."

"Your sympathy," replied the Reed, "is kind,
        And to my mind
Your heart is good; and yet dismiss your thought.
For us, no more than you, the winds are fraught
With danger, for I bend, but do not break.
As yet, a stout resistance you can make,
And never stoop your back, my friend;
But wait a bit, and let us see the end."
Black, furious, raging, swelling as he spoke,
The fiercest wind that ever yet had broke
From the North's caverns bellowed through the sky.
The Oak held firm, the Reed bent quietly down.
The wind blew faster, and more furiously,
      Then rooted up the tree that with its head
Had touched the high clouds in its majesty,
      And stretched far downwards to the realms of dead.

FABLE XXII.

AGAINST THOSE WHO ARE HARD TO PLEASE.

HAD I when born, from fair Calliope
      Received a gift such as she can bestow
Upon her lovers, it should pass from me
To Æsop, and that very soon, I know;
I'd consecrate it to his pleasant lies.
Falsehood and verse have ever been allies;
Far from Parnassus, held in small esteem,
I can do little to adorn his theme,
Or lend a fresher lustre to his song.
I try, that's all—and plan what one more strong
      May some day do—
      And carry through.
Still, I have written, by-the-bye,
The wolf's speech and the lamb's reply.
What's more, there's many a plant and tree
Were taught to talk, and all by me.

Was that not my enchantment, eh?
"Tut! Tut!" our peevish critics say,
"Your mighty work all told, no more is
Than half-a-dozen baby stories.
Write something more authentic then,
And in a higher tone."—Well, list, my men!—
After ten years of war around their towers,
The Trojans held at bay the Grecian powers;
A thousand battles on Scamander's plain,
Minings, assaults, how many a hero slain!
Yet the proud city stoutly held her own,
Till, by Minerva's aid, a horse of wood,
Before the gates of the brave city stood.
Its flanks immense the sage Ulysses hold,
Brave Diomed, and Ajax, churlish, bold;
These, with their squadrons, will the vast machine
Bear into fated Troy, unheard, unseen—
The very gods will be their helpless prey.
Unheard-of stratagem; alas! the day,
That will the workmen their long toil repay.—
"Enough, enough!" our critics quickly cry,
"Pause and take breath; you'll want it presently.
Your wooden horse is hard to swallow,
With foot and cavalry to follow.
Why this is stranger stuff, now, an' you please,
Than Reynard cheating ravens of their cheese;
What's more, this grand style does not suit you well,
That way you'll never bear away the bell."
Well, then, we'll lower the key, if such your will is.—
Pensive, alone, the jealous Amaryllis

AGAINST THOSE WHO ARE HARD TO PLEASE.

Sighed for Alcippus—in her care,
She thinks her sheep and dog alone will share.
Tircis, perceiving her, slips all unseen,
Behind the willows' waving screen,
And hears the shepherdess the zephyrs pray,
To bear her words to lover far away.—
"I stop you at that rhyme,"
    Cries out my watchful critic,
    Of phrases analytic;
"It's not legitimate; it cannot pass this time.
And then I need not show of course,
The line wants energy and force;
    It must be melted o'er again, I say."
You paltry meddler, prate no more,
    I write my stories at my ease.
Easier to sit and plan a score,
    Than such a one as you to please.

        Fastidious men and over wise,
        There's nothing ever satisfies.

FABLE XXIII.

THE COUNCIL HELD BY THE RATS.

A TYRANT Cat, by surname Nibblelard,
    Through a Rat kingdom spread such gloom
By waging war and eating hard,
    Only a few escaped the tomb;
The rest, remaining in their hiding-places,
    Like frightened misers crouching on their pelf,
Over their scanty rations made wry faces,
    And swore the Cat was old King Nick himself.
        One day, the terror of their life
        Went on the roof to meet his wife:
        During the squabbling interview
        (I tell the simple truth to you),
The Rats a chapter called. The Dean,
    A cautious, wise, old Rat,
        Proposed a bell to fasten on the Cat.
"This should be tried, and very soon, I mean;

THE COUNCIL HELD BY THE RATS.

THE COUNCIL HELD BY THE RATS.

So that when war was once begun,
Safe underground their folk could run,—
This was the only thing that could be done."
With the wise Dean no one could disagree;
Nothing more prudent there could be:
The difficulty was to fix the bell!
One said, "I'm not a fool; you don't catch me:"
"I hardly seem to see it!" so said others.
The meeting separated—need I tell,
The end was words—but words. Well, well, my brothers,
There have been many chapters much the same;
Talking, but never doing—there's the blame.
Chapters of monks, not rats—just so!
Canons who fain would bell the cats, you know.

To talk, and argue, and refute,
    The court has lawyers in long muster-roll;
But when you want a man who'll execute,
    You cannot find a single soul.

FABLE XXIV.

THE WOLF PLEADING AGAINST THE FOX BEFORE THE APE.

A WOLF who'd suffered from a thief,
    His ill-conditioned neighbor, Mr. Fox,
Brought up (and falsely, that is my belief)
    Before the Ape, to fill the prisoner's box.
The plaintiff and defendant in this case
        Distract the place
With questions, answers, cries, and boisterous speeches,
        So angry each is.
In an Ape's memory no one saw
An action so entangled as to law.
Hot and perspiring was the judge's face,
He saw their malice, and, with gravity,
Decided thus:—"I know you well of old, my friends,
    Both must pay damages, I see;

THE WOLF PLEADING AGAINST THE FOX BEFORE THE APE.

You, Wolf, because you've brought a groundless charge.
You, Fox, because you stole from him; on that I'll not enlarge."

    The judge was right; it's no bad plan
    To punish rascals how you can.

FABLE XXV.

THE MIDDLE-AGED MAN AND THE TWO WIDOWS.

A MAN of middle age,
    Fast getting grey,
Thought it would be but sage
    To fix the marriage day.
      He had in stocks,
      And under locks,
  Money enough to clear his way.
Such folks can pick and choose; all tried to please
The moneyed man; but he, quite at his ease,
    Showed no great hurry,
    Fuss, nor scurry.
"Courting," he said, "was no child's play."
Two widows in his heart had shares—
  One young; the other, rather past her prime,
By careful art repairs
  What has been carried off by Time.

THE MIDDLE-AGED MAN AND THE TWO WIDOWS.

The merry widows did their best
To flirt and coax, and laugh and jest;
Arranged, with much of bantering glee,
His hair, and curled it playfully.
The eldest, with a wily theft,
Plucked one by one the dark hairs left.
The younger, also plundering in her sport,
    Snipped out the grey hair, every bit.
Both worked so hard at either sort,
    They left him bald—that was the end of it.
"A thousand thanks, fair ladies," said the man;
"You've plucked me smooth enough;
Yet more of gain than loss, so *quantum suff.*,
For marriage now is not at all my plan.
She whom I would have taken t'other day
    To enroll in Hymen's ranks,
Had but the wish to make me go *her* way,
    And not my own;
    A head that's bald must live alone:
For this good lesson, ladies, many thanks."

FABLE XXVI.

THE FOX AND THE STORK.

THE Fox invited neighbor Stork to dinner,
    But Reynard was a miser, I'm afraid;
He offered only soup, and that was thinner
    Than any soup that ever yet was made.
The guest—whose lanky beak was an obstruction,
    The mixture being served upon a plate—
Made countless vain experiments in suction,
    While Reynard feasted at a rapid rate.
The victim, bent upon retaliation,
    Got up a little dinner in return.
Reynard accepted; for an invitation
    To eat and drink was not a thing to spurn.
He reached the Stork's at the appointed hour,
    Flattered the host, as well as he was able,
And got his grinders ready to devour
    Whatever dishes may be brought to table.

THE FOX AND THE STORK.

But, lo! the Stork, to punish the offender,
      Had got the meat cut very fine, and placed
Within a jug; the neck was long and slender,
      Suited exactly to its owner's taste.
The Stork, whose appetite was most extensive,
      Emptied the jug entirely to the drègs;
While hungry Reynard, quite abashed and pensive,
      Walked homewards with his tail between his legs.

      Deceivers reap the fruits of their deceit,
      And being cheated may reform a cheat.

FABLE XXVII.

THE LION AND THE GNAT.

"GO, paltry insect, refuse of the earth!"
    Thus said the Lion to the Gnat one day.
The Gnat held the Beast King as little worth;
Immediate war declared—no joke, I say.
"Think you I care for Royal name?
I care no button for your fame;
An ox is stronger far than you,
Yet oxen often I pursue."
This said; in anger, fretful, fast,
He blew his loudest trumpet blast,
And charged upon the Royal Nero,
Himself a trumpet and a hero.
    The time for vengeance came;
    The Gnat was not to blame.
Upon the Lion's neck he settled, glad
To make the Lion raving mad;

THE LION AND THE GNAT.

THE LION AND THE GNAT.

The monarch foams: his flashing eye
Rolls wild. Before his roaring fly
All lesser creatures; close they hide
To shun his cruelty and pride:
And all this terror at
The bite of one small Gnat,
Who changes every moment his attack,
First on the mouth, next on the back;
Then in the very caverns of the nose,
    Gives no repose.
The foe invisible laughed out,
To see a Lion put to rout;
    Yet clearly saw
    That tooth nor claw
Could blood from such a pigmy draw.
The helpless Lion tore his hide,
And lashed with furious tail his side;
Lastly, quite worn, and almost spent,
Gave up his furious intent.
With glory crowned, the Gnat the battle ground
Leaves, his victorious trump to sound,
As he had blown the battle charge before,
Still one blast for the conquest more.
He flies now here, now there,
To tell it everywhere.
Alas! it so fell out he met
A spider's ambuscaded net,
And perished, eaten in mid-air.

What may we learn by this? why, two things, then:
First, that, of enemies, the smaller men
Should most be dreaded; also, secondly,
That passing through great dangers there may be
Still pitfalls waiting for us, though too small to see.

FABLE XXVIII.

THE ASS LADEN WITH SPONGES, AND THE ASS LADEN WITH SALT.

A PEASANT, like a Roman Emperor bearing
  His sceptre on his shoulder, proudly
Drove his two steeds with long ears, swearing
  At one of them full often and full loudly.
The first, with sponges laden, fast and fleet,
Moved well its feet:
The second (it was hardly its own fault)
Bore bags of salt.
O'er mountain, dale, and weary road,
The weary pilgrims bore their load,
Till to a ford they came one day;
    They halted there
    With wondering air;
The driver knowing very well the way,

Leaped on the Ass the sponges' load that bore,
And drove the other beast before.
That Ass in great dismay
Fell headlong in a hole;
Then plashed and scrambled till he felt
The lessening salt begin to melt;
His shoulders soon had liberty,
And from their heavy load were free.
His comrade takes example from his brother
As sheep will follow one another;
Up to his neck the creature plunges
Himself, his rider, and the sponges;
All three drank deep, the man and Ass
Tipple together many a glass.
The load seemed turned to lead;
The Ass, now all but dead,
Quite failed to gain the bank: his breath
Was gone: the driver clung like death
Till some one came, no matter who, and aid.
Enough, if I have shown by what I've said,
That all can't act alike, you know;
And this is what I wished to show.

THE LION AND THE RAT.

FABLE XXIX.

THE LION AND THE RAT.

IT'S well to please all people when you can;
    There's none so small but one his aid may need
    Here are two fables, if you give good heed,
Will prove the truth to any honest man.

A Rat, in quite a foolish way,
    Crept from his hole between a Lion's paws;
The king of animals showed on that day
    His royalty, and never snapped his jaws.
The kindness was not unrepaid;
Yet, who'd have thought a Lion would need aid
        From a poor Rat?
        Soon after that
The Lion in the forest brake,
In their strong toils the hunters take;
    In vain his roars, his frenzy, and his rage.

LA FONTAINE'S FABLES.

But Mr. Rat runs up; a mesh or two
Nibbles, and lets the Lion through.

    Patience and length of time may sever.
    What strength and empty wrath could never.

FABLE XXX.

THE DOVE AND THE ANT.

THE next example we must get
    From creatures even smaller yet.
A Dove came to a brook to drink,
When, leaning on the crumbling brink,
An Ant fell in, and failed to reach,
Through those vast ocean waves, the beach.
The Dove, so full of charity is she,
Threw down a blade of grass, a promontory,
Unto the Ant, who so once more,
Grateful and glad, escaped to shore.
      Just then passed by
A scampish poacher, soft, bare-footed, came
      Creeping and sly;
A crossbow in his hand he bore:
Seeing the Dove, he thought the game
Safe in the pot and ready for the meal:

Quick runs the Ant, and stings his heel;
The angry rascal turns his head;
The Dove, who sees the scoundrel stoop,
Flies off, and with her flies his soup.

FABLE XXXI.

THE ASTROLOGER WHO LET HIMSELF FALL INTO THE WELL.

TO an Astrologer, who by a blunder
    Fell in a well, said one, "You addle-head,
Blind half an inch before your nose, I wonder
    How you can read the planets overhead."

This small adventure, not to go beyond,
    A useful lesson to most men may be;
How few there are at times who are not fond
    Of giving reins to their credulity,
Holding that men can read,
    In times of need,
The solemn Book of Destiny,
That book, of which old Homer sung.
What was the ancient *chance*, in common sense,
But modern Providence?

LA FONTAINE'S FABLES.

Chance that has always bid defiance
To laws and schemes of human science.
If it were otherwise, a single glance
Would tell us there could be no fortune and no chance.
All things uncertain;
Who can lift the curtain?
    Who knows the will of the Supreme?
He who made all, and all with a design;
    Who but himself can know them? who can dream
He reads the thoughts of the Divine?
Did God imprint upon the star or cloud
The secrets that the night of Time enshroud,
In darkness hid?—only to rack the brains
Of those who write on what each sphere contains.
To help us shun inevitable woes,
And sadden pleasure long before its close;
Teaching us prematurely to destroy,
And turn to evil every coming joy,
This is an error, nay, it is a crime.
The firmament rolls on, the stars have destined time.
The sun gives light by day,
And drives the shadows of the night away.
Yet what can we deduce but that the will Divine
Bids them rise and bids them shine,
To lure the seasons on, to ripen every seed,
    To shed soft influence on men;
What has an ordered universe to do indeed,
    With chance, that is beyond our ken?
Horoscope-makers, cheats, and quacks,
On Europe's princes turn your backs,

THE ASTROLOGER.

And carry with you every bellows-working alchemist:
You are as bad as they, I wist.—
But I am wandering greatly, as I think,
Let's turn to him whom Fate forced deep to drink.
Besides the vanity of his deceitful art,
He is the type of those who at chimeras gape,
Forgetting danger's simpler shape,
And troubles that before us and behind us start.

FABLE XXXII.

THE HARE AND THE FROGS.

ONE day sat dreaming in his form a Hare,
    (And what but dream could one do there?
With melancholy much perplexed
(With grief this creature's often vexed).
"People with nerves are to be pitied,
And often with their dumps are twitted;
Can't even eat, or take their pleasure;
Ennui," he said, "torments their leisure.
See how I live: afraid to sleep,
My eyes all night I open keep.
'Alter your habits,' some one says;
But Fear can never change its ways:
In honest faith shrewd folks can spy,
That men have fear as well as I."
Thus the Hare reasoned; so he kept
Watch day and night, and hardly slept;

THE HARE AND THE FROGS.

THE HARE AND THE FROGS.

Doubtful he was, uneasy ever;
A breath, a shadow, brought a fever.
It was a melancholy creature,
The veriest coward in all nature;
A rustling leaf alarmed his soul,
He fled towards his secret hole.
Passing a pond, the Frogs leaped in,
Scuttling away through thick and thin,
To reach their dark asylums in the mud
"Oh! oh!" said he, "then I can make them scud
As men make me; my presence scares
Some people too! Why, they're afraid of Hares!
  I have alarmed the camp, you see.
Whence comes this courage? Tremble when I come:
  I am a thunderbolt of war, may be;
My footfall dreadful as a battle drum!"

  There's no poltroon, be sure, in any place,
  But he can find a poltroon still more base.

FABLE XXXIII.

THE TWO BULLS AND THE FROG.

TWO Bulls were butting in rough battle,
    For the fair belle of all the cattle;
A Frog, who saw them, shuddering sighed.
"What ails you?" said a croaker by his side.
"What? why, good gracious! don't you see
The end of all this fight will be
That one will soon be chased, and yield
The empire of this flowery field;
And driven from rich grass to feed,
Searching the marsh for rush and reed,
He'll trample many a back and head.
And every time he moves we're dead.
'Tis very hard a heifer should occasion
To us so cruel an invasion."
There was good sense in the old croaker's fear,
For soon the vanquished Bull came near:

THE TWO BULLS AND THE FROG.

Treading with heedless, brutal power,
He crushed some twenty every hour.

The poor in every age are forced by Fate
To expiate the follies of the great.

FABLE XXXIV.

THE PEACOCK COMPLAINING TO JUNO.

THE Peacock to great Juno came:
    "Goddess," he said, "they justly blame.
The song you've given to your bird:
All nature thinks it most absurd,
The while the Nightingale, a paltry thing,
Is the chief glory of the spring : . . . .
Her note so sweet, and deep, and strong.
" I do thee, jealous bird, no wrong,"
    Juno, in anger, cried :
    " Restrain thy foolish pride.
Is it for you to envy others' song?—
You who around your neck art wearing,
Of rainbow silks a hundred different dyes?—
You, who can still display to mortal's eyes,
    A plume that far outfaces
    A lapidary's jewel-cases?

THE PEACOCK COMPLAINING TO JUNO.

THE PEACOCK COMPLAINING TO JUNO.

Is there a bird beneath the skies,
More fit to please and strike?.
No animal has every gift alike:
We've given you each one his special dower;
This one has beauty, and that other power.
Falcons are swift; the Eagle's proud and bold;
By Ravens sorrow is foretold;
The Crow announces miseries to come;
All are content if singing or if dumb.
Cease, then, to murmur, lest, as punishment,
The plumage from thy foolish back be rent."

FABLE XXXV.

THE BAT AND THE TWO WEASELS.

A BAT one day into a Weasel's hole.
    Went boldly; well, it was a special blunder.
The Weasel, hating mice with heart and soul,
    Ran up to eat the stranger—where's the wonder?
"How do you dare," he said, "to meet me here,
When you and I are foes, and always were?
Ain't you a mouse?—lie not, and cast off fear;
You are; or I'm no Weasel: have a care."
    "Now, pardon me," replied the Bat,
    "I'm really anything but that.
What! I a mouse? the wicked tattlers lie.
    Thanks to the Maker of all human things,
    I am a bird—here are my wings:
Long live the cleavers of the sky!"
These arguments seemed good, and so,
The Weasel let the poor wretch go.

THE BAT AND THE TWO WEASELS.

But two days later, though it seems absurd,
The simpleton into another hole intruded.
This second Weasel hated every bird,
And darted on the rash intruder.
"There you mistake," the Bat exclaimed;
"Look at me, ain't I rashly blamed?
What makes a bird; its feathers?—yes.
    I am a mouse—long live the rats,
    And Jupiter take all the cats."
So twice, by his supreme address,
This Bat was saved—thanks to *finesse*.

Many there are who, changing uniform,
    Have laughed at every danger and intrigue;
The wise man cries, to 'scape the shifting storm,
    "Long live the King!" or, "Glory to the League!"

FABLE XXXVI.

THE BIRD WOUNDED BY AN ARROW

A BIRD by well-aimed arrow shot,
    Dying, deplored its cruel lot;
And cried, " It doubles every pain
When from oneself the cause of ruin's ta'en.
Oh, cruel men, from our own wings you drew
The plume that winged the shaft that slew;
But mock us not, you heartless race,
You, too, will some time take our place;
For half at least of Japhet's brothers
Forge swords and knives to slay the others."

FABLE XXXVII.

THE MILLER, HIS SON, AND THE ASS.

THE Arts are birthrights; true, and being so,
    The fable to the ancient Greeks we owe;
But still the field can ne'er be reaped so clean
As not to let the later comers glean.
The world of fiction's full of deserts bare,
Yet still our authors make discoveries there.
Let me repeat a story, good, though old,
That Malherbe to Racan, 'tis rumored, told;
Rivals of Horace, heirs in every way,
Apollo's sons, our masters, I should say:
They met one time in friendly solitude,
Unbosoming those cares that will obtrude.
Racan commences thus,—" Tell me, my friend,
You, who the clue of life, from end to end,
Know well, and step by step, and stage by stage,
Have lost no one experience of age;

LA FONTAINE'S FABLES.

How shall I settle? I must choose my station.
You know my fortune, birth, and education.
Shall I the provinces make my resort,
Carry the colors, or push on at court?
The world has bitterness, and it has charms,
War has its sweets, and marriage its alarms:
Easy to follow one's own natural bent,
But I've both court and people to content."

"Please everybody!" Malherbe says, with crafty eye.
" Now hear my story ere you make reply.
I've somewhere read, a Miller and his Son,
One just through life, the other scarce begun
(Boy of fifteen, if I remember well),
Went one fair day a favorite Ass to sell;
To take him fresh—according to wise rules—
They tied his feet and swung him—the two fools—
They carried him just like a chandelier,
Poor simple rustics (idiots, I fear).
The first who met them gave a loud guffaw,
And asked what clumsy farce it was he saw.
'The greatest ass is not the one who walks,'
So sneeringly the passing horseman talks.
The Miller frees the beast, by this convinced.
The discontented creature brayed and winced
In its own *patois;* for the change was bad:
Then the good Miller mounted the poor lad.
As he limped after, there came by that way
Three honest merchants, who reviling say,
'Dismount! why, that won't do, you lazy lad;
Give up the saddle to your grey-haired dad;

THE MILLER, HIS SON, AND THE ASS.

THE MILLER, HIS SON, AND THE ASS.

You go behind, and let your father ride.'
'Yes, masters,' said the Miller, 'you decide
Quite right; both ways I am content.'
He took his seat, and then away they went.
Three girls next passed: 'Oh, what a shame:' says one,
'A father treating like a slave his son!
The churl rides like a bishop's calf.' 'Not I,'
The Miller made the girls a sharp reply:
'Too old for veal, you hussies, and ill-famed.'
Still with such jesting he became ashamed,
Thought he'd done wrong; and changing his weak mind,
Took up his son upon the croup behind.
But three yards more, a third sour, carping set
Began to cavil,—'Biggest fools we've met!
The beast is done—he'll die beneath their blows.
What! load a poor old servant!' so it grows:
'They'll go to market, and they'll sell his skin.'
'Parbleu!' the Miller said, 'not worth a pin
The fellow's brains who tries with toil and strife
To please the world, his neighbor, and his wife.
But still we'll have a try as we've begun:'
So off the Ass they jumped, himself and son.
The Ass in state goes first, and then came they.
A quidnunc met them—'What! is that the way?
The Ass at ease, the Miller quite foot-sore!
That seems an Ass that's greatly held in store.
Set him in gold—frame him—now, by the mass,
Wear out one's shoes to save a paltry Ass!
Not so went Nicolas his Jeanne to woo;
The song says that he rode to save his shoe.

There go three asses.' Right,' the Miller cries ;
'I am an Ass, it's true, and you are wise ;
But henceforth I don't care, so let them blame
Or praise, no matter, it shall be the same ;
Let them be quiet, pshaw ! or let them tell,
I'll go my own way now ;'" and he did well.

Then follow Mars, or Cupid, or the Court,
Walk, sit, or run, in town or country sport,
Marry or take the cowl, empty or fill the bag,
Still never doubt the babbling tongues will wag.

FABLE XXXVIII.

THE COCK AND THE FOX.

UPON a branch a crafty sentinel,
    A very artful old bird, sat.
"Brother," a Fox said, "greet you well"
    (He speaks so soft—there's guile in that);
"Our quarrel's over, peace proclaimed;
    I bring the news; come down, embrace;
Do not delay; I shall be blamed
    If soon not twenty stages from this place.
Now you and yours can take your ease:
      Do what you please,
      Without a fear;
We're brothers now, you know, my dear.
Light up the bonfires everywhere:
      Dismiss all care;
But let us first, to seal the bliss,
Have one fraternal, tender kiss."

"Friend," said the Cock, "upon my word,
More glorious news I never heard.
    This peace,
    May it increase;
It's double joy to hear it, friend, from thee.
    Ha! there I see
Two greyhounds—couriers, doubtless, as you are—
    Coming fast down yonder scaur:
    They'll be here in a minute,
    Ah! yes, there's something in it—
I'll come down quick:—we'd better kiss all round."
"Adieu," the Fox said: "Sir, my business presses;
We shall meet shortly, I'll be bound:
    Another time we can exult
    Over this end of our distresses."
    Then off the rascal ran to ground,
Full of chagrin and discontent.
The Cock laughed loud, to see his fear,
And clapped his wings, his wives to cheer.

It is a pleasure doubly sweet
To trick the scoundrel and the cheat.

THE FROGS WHO ASKED FOR A KING

FABLE XXXIX.

THE FROGS WHO ASKED FOR A KING.

OF Democrats the Frogs grew tired,
      And unto Monarchy aspired;
Clamor so loud, that from a cloud
Great Jove in pity dropped a King,
Silent and peaceful, all allowed;
And yet he fell with such a splash, the thing
Quite terrified those poor marsh folks,
      Not fond of jokes,
Foolish and timid, all from him hid;
      And each one brushes
To hide in reeds, or sneak in rushes;
And from their swampy holes, poor little souls!
For a long time they dared not peep
At the great giant, still asleep.
      And yet the monarch of the bog
      Was but A LOG,

Whose solemn gravity inspired with awe
The first who venturing saw;
He hobbled somewhat near,
With trembling and with fear;
Then others followed, and another yet,
Until a crowd there met;
At last the daring mob grew bolder,
And leaped upon the royal shoulder;
Good man, he did not take it ill,
But as before kept still.
Soon Jupiter is deafened with the din—
"Give us a king who'll move," they all begin.
The monarch of the gods sends down a Crane,
Who with a vengeance comes to reign.
  He gobbles and he munches,
   He sups and lunches; .
Till louder still the frogs complain.
"Why, see!" great Jupiter replied,
"How foolishly you did decide.
You'd better kept your first—the last is worst.
You must allow, if you are fair,
King Log was calm and *debonnair*:
With him, then, be ye now content,
For fear a third, and worse, be sent."

FABLE XL.

THE DOG AND HER COMPANION.

A DOG, proud of her new-born family,
    And needing shelter for her restless brood,
Begged a snug kennel with such urgency,
    A generous friend at last was found who would
Supply her pressing need—so it was lent.
After a week or so the good soul went
And asked it back.—" Only a fortnight more :"
    The little ones could hardly walk as yet ;
'Twas kindly granted as before.
    The second term expired, again they met:
The friend demands her house, her room, her bed.
This time the graceless dog showed teeth, and scowled ;
" I and my children are prepared to go," she growled.
" If you can put us out and reign instead."
    By this time they were grown,
    And better left alone.

Lend to bad men, and you'll regret it much;
    To draw from them the money right,
    You must plead, and you must fight,
Or else your gold you'll never touch.
    Only the truth I mean to tell:
    Give them an inch, they'll take an ell.

THE FOX AND THE GRAPES.

FABLE XLI.

THE FOX AND THE GRAPES.

A CERTAIN hungry Fox, of Gascon breed
  (Or Norman—but the difference is small),
Discovered, looking very ripe indeed,
  Some Grapes that hung upon an orchard-wall.
Striving to clamber up and seize the prey,
  He found the fruit was not within his power;
"Well, well," he muttered, as he walked away,
  "It's my conviction that those grapes are sour.'

The Fox did wisely to accept his lot;
'Twas better than complaining, was it not?

FABLE XLII.

THE EAGLE AND THE BEETLE.

JOHN RABBIT, by an Eagle followed, fled,
    And in his terror hid his head
In a poor Beetle's hole, that happened to be there.
You well may guess that this poor lair
Was insecure; but where to hide? alack!
He crouched—the Eagle pounced upon his back.
    The friendly Beetle intercedes,
    And, all in tears, he kindly pleads:
"Queen of the Birds! no doubt, in spite of me,
You can this trembling creature bear away;
But spare me this affront, this grief, I pray.
John Rabbit begs his little life of thee;
Grant it for pity's sake, sweet ma'am, now do!"
The bird of Jove disdained to make reply,
But struck the Beetle with her wing—one—two—
Then bore John Rabbit to the upper sky.

THE EAGLE AND THE BEETLE.

Indignant Beetle of revenge in quest,
Flew straight to the proud Eagle's nest;
Broke in her absence all her eggs—the lot—
Her sweetest hopes—the eggs she held so dear.
     Angry people have no fear.
The Eagle, coming to the well loved spot,
And seeing all the hideous fricassee,
Filled Heaven with shrieks; but could not find
On whom to vent her wrath—you see,
Her fury made her blind.
She mourned in vain; that year it was her fate
Childless to be, and desolate.
The next she built a loftier nest—in vain,
The Beetle addled all the eggs again.
John Rabbit's death was well avenged indeed!
For six long months the Eagle's moanings flew,
And woke the echoing forest through.
The bird that bore off Ganymede
Furious and loud remonstrance made,
And flew to Jupiter for aid.
Her eggs she placed upon the Thunderer's lap—
There could come no mishap;
Jove must defend them: who would dare
To touch the objects of his care?
The enemy now changed his note; he soared,
And let some earth fall where they're stored;
The god, his vestment shaking carelessly
Let the eggs fall into infinity.

The Eagle, mad with rage at the event
    (Merely an accident),
Swore she would leave the wicked court,
And make the desert her resort;
    With such vagaries.—
    (In rage all fair is.)
Poor Jupiter in silence heard;
The Beetle came, and charged the bird—
In the tribunal of the upper air
Related the affair.
The god pronounced the Eagle in the wrong,
But still the mutual hate was strong.
To make a truce, Jove then arranged
The time for Eagles' hatching should be changed
To winter, when the marmots sleep,
And Beetles from the daylight keep.

FABLE XLIII.

THE RAVEN WHO WISHED TO IMITATE THE EAGLE.

THE bird of Jove bore off a heavy "mutton;"
    A Raven, witness of the whole affair,
Weaker in back but scarcely less a glutton,
    Resolved to do the same, whate'er
        Might come of it.
        With greedy wit,
Around the flock he made a sweep,
Marking, among the fattest sheep,
        One of enormous size,
        Fit for a sacrifice.
Said Master Raven, winking both his eyes,
"Your nurse's name I cannot tell,
But such fat flesh will suit me well:
You're ready for my eating."
Then on the sheep, slow, sluggish, bleating,

The Raven settled down, not knowing
The beast weighed more than a mere cream-cheese could.
It had a fleece as thickly growing
As beard of Polyphemus—tangled wood—
That clung to either claw; the animal could not withdraw.
The shepherd comes, and calling to his boy,
Gives him the Raven for a toy.

We must take care; the moral is quite clear—
The footpad mustn't rob on the highway.
Example is a dangerous lure, I fear:
Men-eaters are not all great people; no, I say,
Where wasps passed last week gnats are crushed to-day.

THE WOLVES AND THE SHEEP.

FABLE XLIV.

THE WOLVES AND THE SHEEP.

AFTER a thousand years of open war,
    The Wolves signed treaty with their foes, the Sheep:
It seemed to be the best for both, by far;
For if the wolves contrived their tithes to reap,
The shepherds liked a coat of tanned Wolf-skin.
No liberty for pasture had there been,
Neither for carnage; never was there rest!
None could enjoy what pleasures seemed the best;
Peace was concluded—hostages surrendered.
The Wolves their cubs, the Sheep their watch-dogs rendered;
Th' exchange was made in form and order due,
Commissioners were there and not a few;
Some time elapsed, but soon the Wolf-cubs grew
To perfect Wolves, and with a taste for killing;
They chose a time the shepherds were away,
Choked all the fattest lambs that they could slay,

And bore them to the woods; no whit unwilling,
Their fellow-plotters waited for them there.
The dogs, who, full of trust, had thrown by care,
Were slain so quickly, that not one e'en knew
Who their assailants were that bit and slew.
War 'gainst the bad, a war that never ends;
Peace is a wholesome thing, good men are friends.
That I allow; yet peace is but a word, a senseless joke,
With wicked people, and such faithless folk.

FABLE XLV

THE CAT CHANGED INTO A WOMAN.

A MAN loved, heart and soul, his favorite Cat;
    She was his pet, his beauty, and all that.
Her mewing was so sweet, and was so sad:—
He was far madder than the mad.
This man, then, by his tears and praying,
By wizard charms and much soothsaying,
Wrought things so well, that Destiny,
One fine day, changed the Cat into a Woman
        (A change uncommon),
And they were married, soon as they could be.
Mad friends became mad lovers then;
    And not the fairest dame e'er known
    Had ever such affection shown
To him she'd chosen from all men.
The love-blind fool, delighted with his bride,
    Found not a trace of Cat was left at all,

LA FONTAINE'S FABLES.

    No scratch or caterwaul;
He fondles her, she him: she is his pride;
    She is the fairest of her kind,
    A perfect woman, to his mind.
One night some mice came gnawing at the curtain;
It broke the lady's sleep, that's certain;
At once she leaped upon her feet—
To cats revenge is very sweet—
And on all-fours she ran to seize
Those creatures always prone to tease;
But she was changed—in shape and wit—
They did not care for her a bit.
This aberration on her part
Was grief perpetual to his heart.
It never ceased to be the way
Whenever mice were out at play;
For when a certain time has gone,
The jug is seasoned; and the cloth gets wrinkles.
In vain we try to alter what is done,
The warning bell unheeded tinkles.
Things will not change again; one knows
There is no way to end the matter,
Neither by pitchforks nor by blows;
Though Habit you should beat and tatter.
You'll not be master of the place,
Saddle or bridle—how you will;
For if the door's slammed in its face,
It comes back o'er the window-sill.

PHILOMEL AND PROGNE.

FABLE XLVI.

PHILOMEL AND PROGNE.

PROGNE, the Swallow, set forth from her dwelling,
    And, leaving the cities afar, took flight
For the grove that Philomel chose for telling
    Her ancient griefs to the listening night.
"Sister," said Progne, "I have not met you
    For nearly the space of a thousand years.
Why are we parted? I cannot forget you,
    Nor banish our Thracian trials and tears.
Come, leave this wood; it is dark and lonely."
    "What haunt could be pleasanter?" Philomel asked
"And is it," said Progne, "for animals only,
    Or peasants at best, that your efforts are tasked?
With a note so rich 'tis a thousand pities
    To scatter its charms to the desert air.
Come, quit this grove to delight our cities
    And waste no longer a gift so rare.

These woods, my sister, must oft remind you
    Of all the sorrow King Tereus wrought.
Leave, leave the terrible days behind you,
    And give to the past not a tearful thought."
"'Tis the memory, dear, of our Thracian troubles,"
    Said Philomel, sadly, "that bids me stay;
For the sight of humanity only doubles
    The grief of the times that have passed away!"

FABLE XLVII.

THE LION AND THE ASS.

THE King of Animals a *battue* made
      Upon his birthday, bent to fill his bags.
The Lion's game is not with sparrows played;
But boars of bulk, and good-sized, portly stags.
      For an ally in this affair,
      He had an able minister.
The Ass, with Stentor's voice, served as his hunting-horn;
The Lion hid deep 'mid the thickest wood,
And ordered him to bray loud as he could;
So that the clamor shrilly borne,
Might drive from every nook and lair
Those not initiated to the sound.
The hideous tempest came; the air
Shook with the dreadful discord; round
It flew, and scared the fiercest forest creatures;
They fled with terror-stricken features.

And fell into the ready snare,
Where the King Lion stood to meet his prey.
"Have I not served thee brave and true?"
The Ass said, taking to himself the palm.
"Yes," quoth the Lion, grave and calm,
"'Twas nobly brayed; I own to you,
Had I not known your name and race,
I had been almost frightened too!"
Had he been rash, the Ass, his rage
Would not have hidden, I'll engage.
Just was the rallying, though severe;
For who can bear a bragging Ass?
It does not fit their rank or class,
And very ill becomes their business here.

FABLE XLVIII.

THE CAT AND THE OLD RAT.

I'VE read in some old Fabulist, I know,
    A second Nibblelard, of Cats
The Alexander, and of Rats
The Attila, struck many a fatal blow;
And this exterminating creature
Was quite a Cerberus by nature.
(The author writes) For miles away
This cat was feared; he'd vowed, they say,
    To clear the world of mice,
    And in a trice.
The disks within a jar hung gingerly,
"The death to Rats:" the traps, and gins, and springs
The nooses, poisons, and such things,
Were nothing to this Cat, but merely toys.
Soon as he heard no longer stir or noise,
The mice being prisoned in each hole,

Cheek and jowl;
So that it was in vain to hope for prey,
    He tried another "lay."
Shammed death, laid down fast holding by a cord;
A trickster, eager for the horde—
The mice, good folk, deem he is hung
For stealing meat or cheese, tight strung
For scratching some one, or for breaking done.
At last they think the monster's sand is run;
His funeral will be quite a gala day.
Then out they slowly creep,
First one small nose, and then another.
Next a young mouse, then an old brother,
And then they scurry back in fright;
But four step once more to the light,
And lastly all come out to play,
And now begins another sort of treat:
The dead cat falls upon his nimble feet,
Snaps up the slowest, head and tail.
"Ha! ha!" he gobbling cried, "It could not fail,
My *ruse de guerre;* no holes avail
To save these creatures, and I warn them now,
They all will come to the same mouth, I trow."
His prophecy came true—the master of his art,
A second time played well his part.
His fur he whitened o'er with flour,
    That very hour,
  And hid within
  A white meal bin.

THE CAT AND THE OLD RAT.

THE CAT AND THE OLD RAT.

No bad contrivance, every one must own.
The Rats could not leave well alone;
One Rat was wary, shy to venture out,
      And pry about—
Man of the world, and master of *finesse*,
He'd lost his tail in battle, too,
And half a dozen tricks he knew.
"This mass of white may be all sham, I guess,"
He cried, still shunning the Cat's ambuscade:
"Beneath the stuff I fear some trap is laid;
      No matter if it's flour or no,
      It may be so;
But sack or not, still I won't venture near."
'Twas neatly said, his prudence and his fears
I much approve; Experience told him true,
      Suspicion's Safety's mother,
      And Wisdom's foster brother.

FABLE XLIX.

A WILL INTERPRETED BY ÆSOP.

IF what they say of Æsop's truth,
    He was the oracle of Greece indeed;
And all the Areopagus, in sooth,
    Was not so wise. And here, if you would plead
For proof, I'll give one, in a pleasant tale,
My friends and readers to regale.

A certain man had daughters three,
Each of a different turn of mind;
The one a toper, loving company;
The second, fond of all coquetry;
The third a miser, and to save inclined.
The man left them, by will and deed,
As laws municipal decreed,
Half his estate, divided equally;
And to their mother just the same:

A WILL INTERPRETED BY ÆSOP.

But only in her power to claim
When all the daughters had their own
And nothing more but that alone.
The father dead, the daughters ran
To read the will—they were not slow
To con it; yet, do what they can,
They could not understand it—no.
What did he wish?—yes, that's the question
That took a good deal of digestion.
'Each one that had her part, no more,
Should to her mother pay it o'er.'
It was not quite the usual way,
With no gold left, to go and pay:
What meant their worthy father, then?
They run and ask the black-gowned men,
Who turn the case for many days—
Turn it a hundred thousand ways;
Yet, after all, in sheer vexation,
Throw down their wigs in perturbation.
At last the judge advised the heirs
At once to settle the affairs.
As to the widow's part, the counsels say,
A third each sister's bound to pay
Upon demand, unless she choose to take
A life annuity, for quietness' sake,
Beginning from the day her husband died,
   And so they all decide.
Then in three lots they part the whole estate:
In number one the plate;

LA FONTAINE'S FABLES.

The mighty cellars; summer-houses built
    Beneath the vine;
The stores of rich Malvoisin wine;
The spits, the bowls of silver gilt,
And all the tribes of slaves who wait;—
In short, the perfect apparatus
That gives an epicure his social status.
The second lot comprises
All that a flirting girl surprises:
Embroiderer's and many a lady's maid,
Jewels and costly robes;—be sure
The town house, and the furniture,
And stately eunuchs, rich arrayed.
Lot three comprises farming-stock,
Pastures and houses, fold and flock;
Laborers and horses, stores and herds.
This done, they fix, with many words,
That since the lottery won't select
What each one would the most affect,
The eldest have what she likes best,
Leaving the same choice to the rest.
    In Athens it fell out,
    This pleased the motley rout,
    Both great and small.
    The judge was praised by all;
    Æsop alone derided
    The way they had decided.
After much time and pains, they'd gone, he thought,
And set the wishes of the man at nought.

A WILL INTERPRETED BY ÆSOP.

"If the dead came to life," he said,
"Athens aloud he would upbraid.
What! men who cherish subtlety,
To blunder o'er a will so stupidly!"
    Then quickly he divides,
    And thus the sage decides:—
To each he gave the part
Least grateful to her heart:
Pressing on them what they most hate.
To the coquette the cups and bowls
Cherished and loved by thirsty souls;
The toper had the farm; still worse than that,
The miser had the slaves and dresses.
This is the way, Æsop confesses,
To make the sisters alienate
Their shares of the bequeathed estate;
Nor would they longer single tarry,
But run post haste and quickly marry;
So very soon the father's gold, set free,
Would to the mother come, with certainty,
Which was the meaning of the testament.
The people wondered, as they homeward went,
That he alone should have more brains
Than all the lawyers and their trains.

FABLE L.

THE LION IN LOVE.

TO MADEMOISELLE SEVIGNE.

LADY, whose charms were meant to be
    A model for the Graces three;
Lend graciously your gentle ear,
And but one simple fable hear;
You'll see, without profound alarm,
A Lion quelled by Cupid's arm.
Love rules with such a tyranny,
Happy those shunning slavery;
Who the harsh monarch only know
By song and poem, not by blow.
When I dare speak of love to you,
Pardon the fable, no whit true,
That gives me courage to bring it,
Perhaps with more of zeal than wit,
A simple offering, rough and rude,

THE LION IN LOVE.

THE LION IN LOVE.

Of my devoted gratitude.
    In times when animals could speak,
The Lion came intent to seek
Mankind's alliance—wherefore not?
Since beasts had then by nature got
Courage, intelligence, and skill;
A bearing, too, by no means ill.
Now hear what happened, if you will
A Lion of a noble race
Saw in a vale a pretty face,
A shepherdess', understand,
And instantly he claimed her hand.
The father, prudent and pacific,
Preferred a suitor less terrific,
To give his daughter seemed too bad,
Yet how refuse so wild a lad?
If he refused, perhaps there'd be
A marriage still clandestinely.
The maiden liked her dashing wooer,
Her boisterous, reckless, blustering suer,
And, playing with the creature's mane,
Combed it and smoothed it o'er again;
The prudent father, half afraid
To spurn the lover of the maid,
Said, " But my daughter's delicate,
Your claws may hurt your little mate;
And when you fondle and caress.
Lion, you'll tear her and her dress;
Permit me, sir, to clip each paw,

It shall be done without a flaw,
And, by-the-by, in the meanwhile,
Your teeth 'twould be as well to file;
Your kisses then would be less rough,
And hers far sweeter—that's enough."
The Lion, blinded by affection,
Obeyed the artful man's direction;
Toothless and clawless, he grew prouder
(A fortress without guns or powder).
They loosed the mastiff on him soon,
And he was butchered before noon.
O Love! O Love! when bound by you,
Prudence, to thee we say, Adieu!

FABLE LI.

THE FOX AND THE GOAT.

A FOX once travelled, and for company
    His friend, a large-horned Goat, had he,
Who scarce could see an inch beyond his nose,
While Reynard every trick and quibble knows.
Thirst drove these folks, it so befell,
To seek the bottom of a well.
After they'd had their bout of drinking,
Says Reynard, "Comrade, I am thinking
How we can best get out from here;
Put up your feet and horns—no fear—
Rear up against the wall, my friend,
And I'll climb up—our troubles end.
One spring upon your horns will do;
And I once out can rescue you."
"Now, by my beard! I like the plan,"
The other said, "you're one that can;

LA FONTAINE'S FABLES.

Such folks as you see clear through things,
Some never learn the secret springs;
I never should have found it out,
Though I had groped a year about."
The Fox once free, the Goat compelled
To learn a sermon—the text's "patience."
"If Heaven," he said "had only held
It right to give thee and thy dull relations
Half as much sense as beard—
(But then it hasn't, I'm afeard);
Still use your efforts, my dear sir—no perturbations.
  Certain affairs of state
   Will hardly let me longer wait;
In everything 'tis well to mind the end,
In future think of that, my friend."

THE SHEPHERD AND THE SEA.

FABLE LII.

THE SHEPHERD AND THE SEA.

BESIDE his fold, and free from every care,
  A Shepherd, Amphitrite's neighbor, lived for years;
Small was his fortune, yet while skies were fair,
He was contented, vexed by cares nor fears.
At last the treasures cast upon the shore
Tempted the man; he bartered flock and fold,
And sent forth ships to bring him back the more;
But tempests sank the vessels and the gold.
Once more he went to watch the silly sheep,
No longer master as he had been long,
When his own flocks he used to ward and keep,
And poets called him Tircis in their song;
Now he was Pierrot, and that was all.
After some time he, once more well to do,
Had flocks again to answer to his call;
One day when winds were low, and vessels drew

Safely towards the shore and home, the Shepherd stood
Upon the sunny cliff: "Fair nymphs," he cried,
"Seek some one else, I pray you be so good;
Ma foi, you don't catch me with any tide."

This story is not merely meant to please;
It's sober truth, I say, and serves to show
That pence are better if all safe, you know,
Than pounds of promises; when once at ease,
Remain content, and closely shut your ears
To Circe's wiles; resist her wanton smiles.
Ambition and the Sea, avoid them both,
They're full of miseries and racking fears;
For one who wins there's twenty thousand don't.
Rely on that; the winds and thieves are loth
To lose their prey (and trust to them)—they won't.

FABLE LIII.

THE DRUNKARD AND HIS WIFE.

EACH one's his faults, to which he still holds fast,
    And neither shame nor fear can cure the man;
'Tis *apropos* of this (my usual plan),
I give a story, for example, from the past.
A follower of Bacchus hurt his purse,
His health, his mind, and still grew each day worse;
Such people, ere they've run one-half their course,
Drain all their fortune for their mad expenses.
One day this fellow, by the wine o'erthrown,
Had in a bottle left his senses;
His shrewd wife shut him all alone
In a dark tomb, till the dull fume
Might from his brains evaporate.
He woke and found the place all gloom,
A shroud upon him cold and damp,
Upon the pall a funeral lamp.

"What's this?" said he; "my wife's a widow, then!"
On that the wife, dressed like a Fury, came
Mask'd, and with voice disguised, into the den,
And brought the wretched sot, in hopes to tame,
Some boiling gruel fit for Lucifer.
The sot no longer doubted he was dead—
A citizen of Pluto's—could he err?
"And who are you?" unto the ghost he said.
"I'm Satan's steward," said the wife, "and serve the food
For those within this black and dismal place."
The sot replied, with comical grimace,
Not taking any time to think,
"And don't you also bring the drink?"

FABLE LIV.

KING GASTER AND THE MEMBERS.

HAD I but shown a proper loyalty,
    I had begun my book with royalty.
The Belly is a king, it's true,
And in a certain point of view
His wants the other members share.
Well, once to work for him they weary were;
Each one discussed a better plan,—
To live an idle gentleman,
    Like Monsieur Gaster,
    Their lord and master.
"Without us he must feed on air;
We sweat and toil, and groan with care,
For whom? for him alone; we get no good,
And all our thoughts to find him food;
We'll strike, and try his idle trade."
'Twas done as soon as said.

The hands refused to grasp, the legs to walk,
The eyes to open, and the tongue to talk;
Gaster might do whate'er he could.—
'Twas a mistake they soon repent
      With one consent,
The heart made no more blood, and so
The other members cease to glow;
      All wanted strength,
And thus the working men at length
Saw that their idle monarch, in his way,
Toiled for the common weal as well as they.
And this applies to royalty.
It takes and gives with fair equality;
All draw from it their nourishment:
It feeds the artisan, and pays the magistrate,
Gives laborers food, and soldiers subsidies,
     Distributes in a thousand places
     Its sovereign graces;
In fact, supports the State.

Menenius told the story well,
When discord in the senate fell
And discontented Commons taunted it
For having power and treasure, honor, dignity,
While all the care and pain was theirs,
Taxes and imposts, all the toils of war,
The blood, the sorrow, brand and scar.
Without the walls already do they band,
Resolved to seek another land.

KING GASTER AND THE MEMBERS.

Menenius was able,
By this most precious fable,
To bring them safely back
To the old, honest track.

FABLE LV.

THE MONKEY AND THE DOLPHIN.

IT was a custom with the Greeks
    For travellers by sea to take
Monkeys and fancy dogs, whose tricks
Would pastime in fair weather make.
A vessel with such things on deck,
Not far from Athens, went to wreck;
But for the Dolphins all had drowned.
This animal is friend to man:
The fact in Pliny may be found;
So must be true, say what you can.
A Dolphin half the people saves,
Even a Monkey, by-the-by,
He thought a sailor, from the waves
He kindly helped; the creature sly,
Seated upon the Dolphin's back,
Looked very grave and wise; good lack!

THE MONKEY AND THE DOLPHIN.

THE MONKEY AND THE DOLPHIN.

One would have really almost sworn
T'was old Arion, all forlorn.
The two had nearly reached the land,
When just by chance, and such a pity!
Fish asks, "Are you from Athens grand?"
"Yes; oh, they know me in that city;
If you have any business there,
Employ me, for it is truly where
My kinsfolk hold the highest place.
My second cousin is Lord Mayor."
The Dolphin thanked him with good grace:
"And the Piræus knows your face?
You see it often, I dare say?"
"See him! I see him every day;
An old acquaintance; that is so."
The foolish chatterer did not know
Piræus was a harbor, not a man.
Such people, go where'er you can,
You meet within a mile of home,
Mistaking Vaugirard for Rome,
People who chattering dogmatize
Of what has never met their eyes.
The Dolphin laughed, and turning round,
The Monkey saw, and straightway found
He'd saved mere shadow of humanity;
Then plunged again beneath the sea,
And search amid the billows made
For one more worthy of his aid.

FABLE LVI.

THE EAGLE, THE WILD SOW, AND THE CAT.

AN Eagle lodged its young within a hollow tree;
    A Sow lived at the foot; a Cat between the two.
Friendly they were, good neighbors, the whole three,—
Between the mothers there was no to-do.
At last the Cat malignant mischief made;
She climbed up to the Eagle: "Ma'am, our peace
Is ended, death," she says, "is threatening; I'm dismayed.
We perish if our children die; she'll never cease,
That Sow accursed. See! how she grubs and digs,
And mines and burrows, to uproot our oak;
She hopes to ruin us and ours, to feed her pigs
When the tree falls—Madam, it is no joke!
Were there but hopes of saving one,
I'd go and quietly mourn alone."
Thus sowing fear broadcast, she went
With a perfidious intent,

THE EAGLE, THE WILD SOW, AND THE CAT.

To where the sow sat dozily.
"Good friend and neighbor," whispered she,
"I warn you, if you venture forth,
The eagle pounces on your family;
Don't go and spread the thing about,
Or I shall fall a victim to her wrath."
Having here also sown wild fears,
And set her neighbors by the ears,
The Cat into her hole withdrew;
The Eagle after would not fly
To bring home food; the poor Sow, too,
Was still more fearful and more shy.
Fools! not to see that one's first care
Is for one's self to find good fare;
Both stayed at home, still obstinate
To save their young from cruel fate.
The royal bird, she feared the mine;
The Sow, a pounce upon her swine;
Hunger slew all the porcine brood,
And then the eaglets of the wood;
Not one was left—just think of that!
What a relief to Madame Cat!

   A treacherous tongue sows misery
By its pernicious subtlety;
Of all the ills that from Pandora's box arose,
Not one brought half so many woes
As foul Deceit, daughter of Treachery.

FABLE LVII.

THE MISER WHO LOST HIS TREASURE.

IT'S use that constitutes possession wholly;
   I ask those people who've a passion
For heaping gold on gold, and saving solely,
How they excel the poorest man in any fashion?
Diogenes is quite as rich as they.
True Misers live like beggars, people say;
The man with hidden treasure Æsop drew
Is an example of the thing I mean.
In the next life he might be happy, true;
But very little joy in this he knew;
By gold the Miser was so little blessed.
Not its possessor, but by it possessed;
He buried it a fathom underground;
His heart was with it; his delight
To ruminate upon it day and night;
A victim to the altar ever bound.

THE MISER WHO LOST HIS TREASURE.

THE MISER WHO LOST HIS TREASURE.

He seemed so poor, yet not one hour forgot
The golden grave, the consecrated spot:
Whether he goes or comes, or eats or drinks
Of gold, and gold alone, the Miser thinks.
At last a ditcher marks his frequent walks,
      And muttering talks,
Scents out the place, and clears the whole,
      Unseen by any spies.
On one fine day the Miser came, his soul
Glowing with joy; he found the empty nest;
Bursts into tears, and sobs, and cries,
He frets, and tears his thin grey hair;
He's lost what he had loved the best.
A startled peasant passing there
Inquires the reason of his sighs.
"My gold! my gold! they've stolen all."
"Your treasure! what was it, and where?"
"Why, buried underneath this stone."
      (A moan!)
"Why, man, is this a time of war?
Why should you bring your gold so far?
Had you not better much have let
The wealth lie in a cabinet,
Where you could find it any hour
      In your own power?"
"What! every hour? a wise man knows
Gold comes but slowly, quickly goes;
I never touched it." "Gracious me!"
Replied the other, "why, then, be

LA FONTAINE'S FABLES.

So wretched? for if you say true,
You never touched it, plain the case:
Put back that stone upon the place,
'Twill be the very same to you."

FABLE LVIII.

THE GOUT AND THE SPIDER.

WHEN Mischief made the Spider and the Gout,
"My daughters," said she, "you may clearly vaunt
That nowhere in a human haunt
Are there two plagues more staunch and stout;
Come, choose your dwellings where you would abide:
Here are the hovels—narrow, dark, and poor,
And there the palaces all gilt with pride.
You have your choice—now, what can I say more?
    Here is the lottery prescribed by law,
      Come, daughters, draw."
"The hovel's not my place," the Spider says;
Her sister hates the palace, for the Gout
Sees men called doctors creeping in and out,
They would not leave her half an hour at ease:
She crawls and rests upon a poor man's toe,
      Just so,

LA FONTAINE'S FABLES.

And says, "I shall now do whate'er I please.
No struggles longer with Hippocrates!
No call to pack and march, no one can displace me."
The Spider camps upon a ceiling high,
As if she had a life-long lease, you see
And spins her web continually,
      Ready for any fly.
A servant soon, to clean the room,
Sweeps down the product of her loom.
With each tissue the girl's at issue:
Spiders, busy maids will swish you!
The wretched creature every day
Was driven from her home away;
At last, quite wearied, she gave out,
And went to seek her sister, Gout,
Who in the country mourned her wretched fate:
A thousand times more hopeless her estate;
Even more miseries betide her
Than the misfortunes of the Spider.
Her host had made her dig and hoe,
And rake and chop, and plough and mow,
Until he's all but well.
"I can't resist him. Ah! *ma belle:*
Let us change places." Gladly heard,
The Spider took her at her word.
In the dark hovel she can spin:
No broom comes there with bustling din.
The Gout, on her part, pleased to trudge,
Goes straightway—wise as any judge—

THE GOUT AND THE SPIDER.

Unto a bishop, and with whims
So fetters his tormented limbs,
That he from bed can never budge.
       Spasms!
       Cataplasms!
Heaven knows, the doctors make the curse
Steal steadily from bad to worse.
Both sisters gloried in the change,
And never after wished to range.

FABLE LIX.

THE EYE OF THE MASTER.

A STAG sought refuge from the chase
   Among the oxen of a stable,
Who counselled him—if he was able—
To find a better hiding-place.
" My brothers," said the fugitive,
" Betray me not; and I will show
The richest pastures that I know;
Your kindness you will ne'er regret;
With interest I'll pay the debt."
The oxen promised well to keep
The secret: couched for quiet sleep,
Safe in a tranquil privacy,
The Stag lay down, and breathed more free.
At even-time they brought fresh hay,
As was their custom day by day;
Men went and came, ah! very near,

THE EYE OF THE MASTER.

THE EYE OF THE MASTER.

And last of all the overseer,
Yet carelessly, for horns nor hair
Showed that the hiding stag was there.
The forest dweller's gratitude
Was great, and in a joyous mood
He waited till the labor ceased,
And oxen were from toil released,
Leaving the exit once more free,
To end his days of slavery.
A ruminating bullock cried,
"All now goes well; but woe betide
When that man with the hundred eyes
Shall come, and you, poor soul! surprise?
I fear the watchful look he'll take,
And dread his visit for your sake;
Boast not until the end, for sure
Your boasting may be premature."
He had not time to utter more,
The master opened quick the door.
"How's this, you rascal men?" said he;
"These empty racks will never do!
Go to the loft; this litter, too,
Is not the thing. I want to see
More care from those that work for me;
Whose turn these cobwebs to brush out?
These collars, traces?—look about!"
Then, gazing round, he spies a head,
Where a fat ox should be instead;
The frightened stag they recognize.

In vain the tears roll from his eyes;
They fall on him with furious blows,
Each one a thrust, until, to close,
They kill and salt the wretched beast
And cook him up for many a feast.

    Phædrus hath put it pithily,
The master's is the eye for me,
The lover's, too, is quick to see.

FABLE LX.

THE WOLF AND THE STORK.

WOLVES are too prone to play the glutton.
    One, at a certain feast, 'tis said,
Fell with such fury on his mutton,
He gave himself quite up for dead,
For in his throat a bone stuck fast.
A Stork, by special stroke of luck,
As he stood speechless, came at last.
He beckoned, and she ran to aid,
    No whit afraid.
A surgeon, and a very friend in need,
She drew the bone out. For the cure she made
She simply asked her fee.
"Fie!" said the Wolf, "you jeer at me,
My worthy gossip. Only see:
What! is it not enough that, sound and safe,

You drew your neck back from my gullet,
　　My pretty pullet?
You are ungrateful. Now, then, go;
Beware, another time, my blow."

FABLE LXI.

THE LION DEFEATED BY MAN.

A PICTURE was exhibited, one day,
    In which an artisan had sought
To paint a lion which had fought,
And had been beaten in the fray.
The passers-by were full of self-applause.
A Lion who looked on reproached the crowd:
"Yes, here I see," he said, "the victory is man's:
The artisan had his own plans;
But if my brothers painted, they'd be proud
To show you man prostrate beneath our claws."

FABLE LXII.

THE SWAN AND THE COOK.

IN a menagerie a Swan and Goose
    Lived like sworn friends, in peace and amity.
This one was meant to please the master's eye,
The other fitted for his palate's use:
This for the garden, that one for the board.
The chateau's fosse was their long corridor,
Where they could swim, in sight of their liege lord,
Splash, drink, and paddle, or fly o'er and o'er,
Unwearied of their pastime, down the moat.
One day the Cook, taking a cup too much,
Mistook the birds, and, seizing by the throat,
Was just about to kill—his blindness such—
The helpless Swan, and thrust him in the pot.
The bird began to sing his dying song:
    The Cook, in great surprise,
    Opened his sleepy eyes.

THE SWAN AND THE COOK.

"What do I do?" he said; "I had forgot:
No, no, Jove willing! may my neck be strung,
Before I kill a bird that sings so well."

Thus, in the dangers that around us throng,
Soft words are often useful, as it here befell.

FABLE LXIII.

THE WOLF, THE GOAT, AND THE KID.

THE She-Goat, going out to feed
  Upon the young grass in the mead,
Closed not the latch until she bid
Her youngest born, her darling kid,
Take care to open door to none,
Or if she did, only to one
Who gave the watchword of the place—
"Curse to the Wolf and all his race!"
The Wolf was just then passing by,
And having no bad memory,
Laid the spell by, a perfect treasure,
Ready to be used at leisure.
The Kid, so tender and so small,
Had never seen a wolf at all.
The mother gone, the hypocrite
Assumes a voice demure and fit—

THE WOLF, THE GOAT, AND THE KID.

"The Wolf be cursed! come, pull the latch."
The Kid says, peeping through a chink,
"Show me a white foot" (silly patch),
"Or I'll not open yet the door, I think."
White paws are rare with wolves—not yet in fashion
The Wolf surprised, and dumb with secret passion,
Went as he came, and sneaked back to his lair:
The Kid had lost her life without that care;
Had she but listened to the word
The watchful Wolf had overheard.
Two sureties are twice as good as one,
Without them she had been undone.
    And so I boldly say,
That too much caution's never thrown away.

FABLE LXIV.

THE WOLF, THE MOTHER, AND THE CHILD.

THIS Wolf recalls another to my mind—
    A friend who found Fate more unkind—
Caught in a neater way, you'll see;
He perished—here's the history:
A peasant dwelt in a lone farm;
The Wolf, his watch intent to keep,
Saw in and out, not fearing harm.
Slim calves and lambs, and old fat sheep,
And regiment of turkeys strutting out;
In fact, good fare was spread about.
The thief grew weary of vain wishes
      For dainty dishes;
But just then heard an Infant cry,
The mother chiding angrily—
      "Be quiet!
      No riot;

THE WOLF, THE MOTHER, AND THE CHILD.

THE WOLF, THE MOTHER, AND THE CHILD.

Or to the Wolf I'll give you, brat!"
The Wolf cried, "Now, I quite like that;"
And thanked the gods for being good.
The Mother, as a mother should,
Soon calmed the child. "Don't cry, my pet!
If the Wolf comes, we'll kill him, there!"
"What's this?" the thief was in a fret;
"First this, then that, there's no truth anywhere;
  I'm not a fool, you know,
   And yet they treat me so.
Some day when nutting, it may hap
I may surprise the little chap."
As these reflections strike the beast,
A mastiff stops the way, at one fierce bound,
To any future feast,
And rough men gird him round.
"What brought you here?" cries many a one;
He told the tale as I have done.
"Good Heavens!" loud the Mother cried;
"You eat my boy! what! darling here
To stop your hunger? Hush! my dear."
They killed the brute and stripped his hide;
His right foot and his head in state
Adorn the Picard noble's gate;
And this was written underneath
The shrivelled eyes and grinning teeth—
"Good Master Wolves, believe not all
That mothers say when children squall."

FABLE LXV.

THE LION GROWN OLD.

A LION, once the terror of the plain
   (Borne down with age, and weakened by decay),
Against rebellious vassals fought in vain,
And found his foes the victors of the fray.
The Horse advanced and gave his king a kick—
The Wolf a bite—the Ox a brutal butt:
Meanwhile the Lion, worn, and sad, and sick,
Could scarce resent this, the "unkindest cut."
But when an Ass came running to the place,
The monarch murmured, with his latest breath,
"Enough! I wished to die, but this disgrace
Imparts a twofold bitterness to death."

FABLE LXVI.

THE DROWNED WOMAN.

I AM not one of those who coolly say,
  "It's nought but just a woman who is drowned!"
I say it's much, yes, much in every way.
The sex I reverence. Taking them all round,
They are the joy of life; then let their praise resound.
And these remarks are really *apropos*:
My fable treating of a woman lost
In a deep river. Ill luck willed it so.
Her husband sought her, at each ford she'd crossed,
To place her body in a fitting tomb.
And as he wandered by the fatal shore
Of the swift stream that bore his wife away,
The people passing he asked o'er and o'er
If they had seen her on that luckless day.
They'd not e'en heard of his sad loss before.
"No," said the first; but seek her lower down:

Follow the stream, and you will find her yet."
Another answered: "Follow her! no, no; that's wrong.
Go further up, and she'll be there, I bet,
Whether the current's weak, or the tide strong.
    It's my conviction,
Such is a woman's love of contradiction,
She'll float the other way your soul to fret."
The raillery was out of season;
And yet the heedless boor had reason,
For such is woman's humor still,
To follow out her own good will;
Yes, from her very birthday morn
Till to the churchyard she is borne,
She'd contradict to her last breath,
And wish she could e'en after death.

FABLE LXVII.

THE WEASEL IN THE GRANARY.

ONCE Madame Weasel, slender-waisted, thin,
    Into a granary, by a narrow chink,
Crept, sick and hungry; quick she glided in,
To eat her fill, and she was wise, I think.
      There at her ease,
      No fear of fees,
She gnawed, and nibbled:—gracious, what a life!
The bacon melted in the strife.
      Plump and rotund she grew,
      As fat as two.
      A week was over,
      Spent in clover.
But one day, when she'd done—and that not badly—
      A noise alarmed her sadly.
She tried the hole she'd entered, wishing to retreat;
      'Twas no such easy feat.

Was she mistaken?—no, the selfsame door:
    She tried it o'er and o'er.
"Yes, yes," she said, "it is the place, I know;
I passed here but a week ago."
A Rat who saw her puzzled, slyly spoke—
"Your pouch was emptier then, before your fast you broke.
Empty you came, and empty you must quit:
I tell you what I've told a dozen more.
But don't perplex the matter, I implore;
They differed from you in some ways, I do admit."

FABLE LXVIII.

THE LARK AND HER LITTLE ONES WITH THE OWNER OF A FIELD.

"DEPEND upon yourself alone,"
    Is a sound proverb worthy credit.
In Æsop's time it was well known,
And there (to tell the truth) I read it.
The larks to build their nests began,
When wheat was in the green blade still—
That is to say, when Nature's plan
Had ordered Love, with conquering will,
To rule the earth, the sea, and air,
Tigers in woods, sea monsters in the deep;
    Nor yet refuse a share
To larks that in the cornfields keep.
One bird, however, of these last,
Found that one-half the spring was past,
Yet brought no mate, such as the season sent

To others. Then with firm intent
Plighting her troth, and fairly matched,
She built her nest and gravely hatched.
All went on well, the corn waved red
Above each little fledgling's head,
Before they'd strength enough to fly,
And mount into the April sky.
A hundred cares the mother lark compel
To seek with patient care the daily food;
But first she warns her restless brood
To watch, and peep, and listen well,
And keep a constant sentinel;
"And if the owner comes his corn to see,
His son, too, as 'twill likely be,
Take heed, for when we're sure of it,
And reapers come, why, we must flit."
No sooner was the Lark away
Than came the owner with his son.
"The wheat is ripe," he said, "so run,
And bring our friends at peep of day,
Each with his sickle sharp and ready."
The Lark returns: alarm already
Had seized the covey. One commences—
"He said himself, at early morn
His friends he'd call to reap the corn."
The old Lark said—"If that is all,
My worthy children, keep your senses;
No hurry till the first rows fall.
We'll not go yet, dismiss all fear;

THE LARK AND HER LITTLE ONES.

THE LARK AND HER LITTLE ONES.

To-morrow keep an open ear.
Here's dinner ready, now be gay."
They ate and slept the time away.
The morn arrives to wake the sleepers,
Aurora comes, but not the reapers.
The Lark soars up: and on his round
The farmer comes to view his ground.
"This wheat," he said, "ought not to stand;
Our friends are wrong no helping hand
To give, and we are wrong to trust
Such lazy fools for half a crust,
Much less for labor. Sons," he cried,
" Go, call our kinsmen on each side;
We'll go to work." The little Lark
Grew more afraid. "Now, mother, mark,
The work within an hour's begun."
The mother answered—"Sleep, my son;
We will not leave our house to-night."
Well, no one came; the bird was right.
The third time came the master by:
"Our error's great," he said, repentantly:
" No friend is better than oneself;
Remember that, my boy, it's worth some pelf.
    Now, what to do?
    Why, I and you
Must whet our sickles and begin;
That is the shortest way, I see;
I know at last the surest plan:
We'll make our harvest as we can."

No sooner had the Lark o'erheard—
" 'Tis time to flit, my children ; come,
Cried out the very prudent bird.
Little and big went fluttering, rising,
Soaring in a way surprising,
And left without a beat of drum.

FABLE LXIX.

THE FLY AND THE ANT.

THE Fly and Ant once quarrelled seriously:
   "O Jupiter!" the first exclaimed, "how vanity
Blinds the weak mind! This mean and crawling thing
Actually ventures to compare
With me, the daughter of the air.
The palace I frequent, and on the board
I taste the ox before our sovereign lord;
While this poor, paltry creature lives for days
On the small straw she drags through devious ways.
Come, Mignon, tell me plainly now,
Do you camp ever on a monarch's brow,
Or on a beauty's cheek? Well, I do so,—
And on her bosom, too, I'd have you know.
I sport among her curls, I place
Myself upon her blooming face.
The ladies bound for conquest go

LA FONTAINE'S FABLES.

To us for patches; their necks' snow
With spots of blackness well contrast,
Of all her toilette cares the last.
Come, now, good fellow, rack your brain,
And let us hear of sense some grain."
"Well, have you done?" replied the Ant
"You haunt kings' palaces, I grant;
But then, by every one you're cursed.
It's very likely you taste first
The gods' own special, sacred feast;
Nor is it better, sir, for that.
The fane you enter, with the train—
So do the godless and profane.
On heads of kings or dogs, 'tis plain,
You settle freely when not wanted,
And you are punished often—granted.
You talk of patches on a belle;
I, too, should patch them just as well.
The name your vanity delights,
Frenchmen bestow on parasites;
Cease, then, to be so grossly vain;
Your aspirations, Miss, restrain;
Your namesakes are exiled or hung,
And you with famine will be clung.
With cold and freezing misery,
Will come your time of penury,
When our King Phœbus goes to cheer
And rule the other hemisphere:
But I shall live upon my store,

THE FLY AND THE ANT.

My labors for the summer o'er,
Nor over mountains and seas go,
Through storm and rain, and drifting snow;
No sorrow near me will alloy
The fulness of the present joy;
Past trouble bars out future care,
True, not false, glory is our share;
And this I wish to show to you—
Time flies, and I must work.   Adieu!
This idle chattering will not fill
My little granary and till."

FABLE LXX.

THE GARDENER AND HIS MASTER.

AN amateur of flowers—bourgeois and yet clown—
    Had made a garden far from any town;
Neat, trim, and snug, it was the village pride;
Green quickset hedges girt its every side;
There the rank sorrel and the lettuce grew,
And Spanish jasmine for his Margot, too,
Jonquils for holidays, and crisp, dry thyme;
But all this happiness, one fatal time,
Was marrèd by a hare; his grief and woe
Compel the peasant to his lord to go.
"This cursed animal," he says, "by night
And day comes almost hourly for his bite;
He spurns my cunning, and defies my snares,
For stones and sticks he just as little cares;
He is a wizard, that is very sure,
And for a wizard is there, sir, a cure?"

THE GARDENER AND THE MASTER.

"Wizard, be hanged!" the lord said; "you shall see
His tricks and wiles will not avail with me;
I'll scare the rascal, on my faith, good man."
"And when?" "To-morrow; I have got a plan."
The thing agreed, he comes with all his troop.
"Good! let us lunch—fowls tender in the coop?
That girl your daughter? come to me, my dear!
When you betroth her, there's a brave lad here.
I know, good man, the matrimonial curse
Digs plaguey deep into a father's purse."
The lord, so saying, nearer draws his chair,
Plays with the clusters of the daughter's hair,
Touches her hand, her arm, with gay respect,
Follies that make a father half suspect
Her coyness is assumed; meantime they dine,
Squander the meat, play havoc with the wine.
"I like these hams, their flavor and their look."
"Sir, they are yours." "Thanks: take them to my cook."
He dined, and amply; his retainers, too;
Dogs, horses, valets, all well toothed, nor few;
My lord commands, such liberties he takes,
And fond professions to the daughter makes.
The dinner over, and the wine passed round,
The hunters rise, and horns and bugles sound;
They rouse the game with such a wild halloo,
The good man is astonished at the crew;
The worst was that, amid this noise and clack,
The little kitchen garden went to wrack.
Adieu the beds! adieu the borders neat!

Peas, chicory, all trodden under feet.
Adieu the future soup!   The frightened hare
Beneath a monster cabbage made his lair.
They seek him—find him; " After him, my boys!"
He seeks the well-known hole with little noise;
Yet not a hole, rather a wound they made
In the poor hedge with hoof and hunting-blade.
" By the lord's orders it would never do
To leave the garden but on horseback, no."
The good man says, " Royal your sports may be;
Call them whate'er you like, but pity me;
Those dogs and people did more harm to-day
Than all the hares for fifty years, I say."

FABLE LXXI.

THE WOODMAN AND MERCURY.

TO M. THE COUNT DE B——

YOUR taste has always been to me a guide;
   I've sought in many ways to win your vote:
Fastidious cares you often would deride,
Forbade me on vain ornament to dote.
I think with you an author wastes his days
Who tries with over-care his tale to tell;
Yet, it's not wise to banish certain traits
Of subtle grace, that you and I love well.
With Æsop's aim, I simply do my best;
And fail—well, just as little as I can.
Try to instruct by reasoning or jest;
No fault of mine if no one likes my plan.
Rude strength is not by any means my forte;
I seek to pelt, with playful ridicule,
Folly and vice; and tease the motley fool

LA FONTAINE'S FABLES.

With stinging missiles—any way, in short;
Not having brawny arms like Hercules.
That is my only talent, that I know.
I have no strength to stem the angry seas,
Or set all honest people in a glow.
Sometimes I try to paint in fabled guise,
A foolish vanity, with envy blended;
Two of life's pivots, mocked at by the wise,
In satires long ago, and not yet ended.
Such was the miserable creature,
Mean and poor in shape, in feature,
That tried to puff herself into and ox.
Sometimes I try, by playful paradox,
To pair a vice with virtue, folly with good sense,
Lambs with gaunt wolves, the ant to match the fly;
Everywhere laughing at the fool's expense,
I mould my work into a comedy,
With countless acts, the universe its scene,
Boundless as the blue serene.
Men, gods, and brutes each play their part,
With more or less of truth and art.
Jove like the rest—come, Mercury;
Ah! look; why, there he comes, I see;
The messenger who's wont to bear
Jove's frequent errands to the fair—
But more of that another day.

   A Woodman's axe had gone astray,
The winner of his bread was gone;

THE WOODMAN AND MERCURY.

THE WOODMAN AND MERCURY.

And he sat moaning all alone.
He had no wealth to buy such things:
The axe his clothes and dinner brings.
Hopeless, and in a murky place,
He sat; the tears ran down his face.
"My own, my poor old axe! Ah! me,
Great Jupiter, I pray to thee;
But give it back from down below,
And I will strike for thee a blow."
His prayer was in Olympus heard;
Mercury entered at the word.
"Your hatchet is not lost," said he;
"But will you know it when you see?
I found an axe, just now, hard by."
A golden axe he presently
Showed to the honest man; but "Nay"
Was all the fellow cared to say.
Next one of silver he refused;
Silver or gold he never used.
Then one of simple steel and wood;
"That's mine!" he cried. "Ah! thankee—good;
I'm quite content with this, you see."
"Come," said the god, "then take the three—
That's my reward for honesty."
"In that case, then, I am content,"
The rustic said, and off he went.
The rumor buzzed the country through,
Soon others lost their axes, too;
And shouting prayers unto the sky,

Jove Mercury sent, to make reply.
To each he showed an axe of gold—
Who but a fool could it behold,
And not say when he saw it shine—
"Hurrah! that's it—yes, that is mine?"
But Mercury gave each rogue instead
A heavy thump upon the head.

He who with simple truth's content,
Will never of his choice repent:
To tell a lie for interest
Was never yet of ways the best.
What does it profit thus to stoop?
Jove is not made an easy dupe.

FABLE LXXII.

THE ASS AND THE LITTLE DOG.

To ape a talent not your own
    Is foolish; no one can affect a grace.
A blundering blockhead better leave alone
The gallant's bows, and tricks, and smiling face.
To very few is granted Heaven's dower—
Few have infused into their life the power
To please, so better far to leave the charm
To them. And may I ask you, where's the harm?
One would not bear resemblance to the Ass,
Who, wishing to be dearer to his master,
Amiably went to kiss him; so it came to pass
There followed instantly no small disaster.
"What!" said he, "shall this paltry thing
Assume by dint of toadying,
Win Madam's friendly fellowship,
And twist and gambol, fawn and skip,

While I have only blows? no, no!
What does he do?—why, all fools know—
He gives his paw; the thing is done,
And then they kiss him every one.
If that is all, upon my word,
To call it difficult's absurd."
Full of this glorious thought, one luckless day,
Seeing his master smiling pass that way,
The clumsy creature comes, and clumsily
Chucks with his well-worn hoof quite gallantly
His master's chin; to please him still the more,
With voice, so sweet, sonorous brays his best.
"Oh, what caresses, and what melody!"
The master cries; ' Ho! Martin, come, be quick!
And, Martin, bring the heaviest stick!"
Then Martin comes; the donkey changed his tune,
   So ended the brief comedy
   In bitter blows and misery.
Donkeys' ambitions pass so soon.

FABLE LXXIII.

MAN AND THE WOODEN IDOL.

A CERTAIN Pagan had a god of wood—
   Deaf was the idol, yet had ears enough;
The Pagan promised to himself much good.
It cost as much as three men; for his fears
Induced repeated vows and offerings;
Fat oxen crowned with garlands and such things.
Never an idol—think of that—
Boasted of victims half as fat.
Yet all this worship brought no grace,
Treasure or legacy, or luck at play;
What's more, if any single storm came near the place,
This man was sure to have to pay;
Yet all the time the god dined well. Now, was this fair?
At last, impatient at the costly care,
He takes a crowbar and the idol smashes
       (Crashes).

Forth comes a stream of gold.
"I feasted you with offerings manifold,
And you were never worth an obolus to me;
Now leave," he said, "my hospitality;
Seek out another altar.   I hold thee
One of those gross and stupid creatures,
With wicked and untoward natures,
Whose gratitude can never grow;
But after many a heavy blow,
The more I gave the less I got; I own
It's very well I changed my tone."

FABLE LXXIV.

THE JAY DRESSED IN PEACOCK'S PLUMES.

A PEACOCK, having moulted, the sly Jay
    Put on the thrown-off plumage with delight;
Amongst some other Peacocks found his way,
And thought himself a fascinating sight.
At last the would-be beau got recognized,
A charlatan, in borrowed plumes equipt—
And laughed at, scouted, hustled, and despised,
Of all his second-hand attire got stript;
Returning to his friends, abashed and poor,
They most politely showed him to the door.

Two-footed Jays are anything but rare,
Who live on facts and fancies not their own;
But these are, luckily, not my affair,
So let me leave the plagiarists alone.

FABLE LXXV.

THE LITTLE FISH AND THE FISHERMAN.

A LITTLE Fish will larger grow, in time,
   If God will only grant him life; and yet
To let him free out of the tangling net
Is folly; and I mean it, though I rhyme:
The catching him again is not so sure, *c'est tout*.
A little Carp, who half a summer knew,
Was taken by an angler's crafty hook.
"All count," the man said; "this begins my feast:
I'll put it in my basket." "Here, just look!"
Exclaimed, in his own way, the tiny beast.
"Now, what on earth can you, sir, want with me?
I'm not quite half a mouthful, as you see.
Let me grow up, and catch me when I'm tall,
Then some rich epicure will buy me dear;
But now you'll want a hundred, that is plain,
     Aye, and as much again.

THE LITTLE FISH AND THE FISHERMAN.

THE LITTLE FISH AND THE FISHERMAN.

To make a dish; and what dish, after all?
Why, good for nothing." "Good for nothing, eh?
Replied the Angler. "Come, my little friend,
Into the pan you go; so end.
Your sermon pleases me, exceedingly.
    To-night we'll try
    How you will fry."

The present, not the future, tense
Is that preferred by men of sense.
The one is sure that you have got:
The other, verily, is not.

FABLE LXXVI.

BATTLE BETWEEN THE RATS AND WEASELS

THE Weasel nation, like the Cats,
    Are always fighting with the Rats;
And did the Rats not squeeze their way
Through doors so narrow, I must say,
The long-backed creatures would slip in,
And swallow all their kith and kin.
One certain year it did betide,
When Rats were greatly multiplied,
Their king, illustrious Ratapon,
His army to the field led on.
The Weasels, too, were soon arrayed,
And the old flag again displayed.
If Fame reported just and true,
Victory paused between the two;
Till fallows were enriched and red
With blood the rival armies shed;

THE RATS AND THE WEASELS.

But soon in every place
Misfortune met the Rattish race.
The rout was so complete, the foe
More dreadful grew at every blow;
And what avails brave Artapax,
Meridarpax, Psicarpax?
Who, covered both with dust and gore,
Drove back the Weasels thrice and more.
Till driven slowly from the plain,
E'en their great courage proved in vain
'Twas Fate that ruled that dreadful hour:
Then each one ran who had the power;
Soldier and captain, jostling fled,
But all the princes were struck dead;
The private, nimble in his feet,
Unto his hole made snug retreat.
The noble, with his lofty plume,
Found that he had by no means room.
To strike with terror—yes, or whether
A mark of honor—rose the feather,
That led to much calamity,
As very soon the nobles see;
Neither in cranny, hole, or crack,
Was space found for the pluméd pack.
In the meantime, the populace
Found access to each lurking-place,
So that the largest heap of slain
From the Rat noblemen is ta'en.

    A nodding feather in the cap

Is oftentimes a great mishap;
A big and over-gilded coach
Will sometimes stop up an approach;
The smaller people, in most cases,
Escape by unregarded places :
Men soon are on great people's traces.

FABLE LXXVII.

THE CAMEL AND THE DRIFT-WOOD.

THE first who saw a real live Camel
    Ran for his life; the second ventured near;
The third, with ready rope, without a fear,
Made a strong halter the wild thing to trammel.
Habit has power to quickly change
Things that at first seem odd and strange;
Stale they grow, and quickly tame,
And hardly seem to be the same.
And, since the question's open, once there stood
A look-out watching all the distant flood;
And seeing something far off on the ocean,
Could not conceal his notion
It was a man-of-war; a moment past,
It turned a fire ship, all ataut and brave,
Then a big boat, and next a bale, and last
Some mere drift timber jostling on the wave.

LA FONTAINE'S FABLES.

How many things watched by the world agree
In this—that far away you see
That there is something, yet when sought,
And seen still nearer, it proves nought.

FABLE LXXVIII.

THE FROG AND THE RAT.

MERLIN said well, that those who often cheat
    Will sometimes cheat themselves—the phrase is old.
I'm sorry that it is, I must repeat
It's full of energy, and sound as gold.
But to my story: once a well-fed Rat,
Rotund and wealthy, plump and fat,
Not knowing either Fast or Lent,
Lounging beside a marsh pool went.
A Frog addressed him in the Frog's own tongue,
And asked him home to dinner civilly.
No need to make the invitation long.
He spoke, however, of the things he'd see:
The pleasant bath, worth curiosity;
The novelties along the marsh's shore;
    The score and score
Of spots of beauty, manners of the races,

LA FONTAINE'S FABLES.

The government of various places,
Some day he would recount with glee
Unto his youthful progeny;
One thing alone the gallant vexed,
And his adventurous soul perplexed;
He swam but little, and he needed aid.
The friendly Frog was undismayed;
His paws to hers she strongly tied,
And then they started side by side.
The hostess towed her frightened guest
Quick to the bottom of the lake—
Perfidious breach of law of nations—
All promises she faithless breaks,
And sinks her friend to make fresh rations.
Already did her appetite
Dwell on the morsel with delight,
   Lunch,
    Scrunch!
He prays the gods; she mocks his woe;
He struggles up; she pulls below.
And while this combat is fought out,
A Kite that's seeking all about
Sees the poor Rat that's like to drown,
And pounces swift as lightning down.
The Frog tied to him, by the way,
Also became the glad Kite's prey;
They gave him all that he could wish,
A supper both of meat and fish.

THE FROG AND THE RAT.

So oftentimes a base deceit
Falls back upon the father cheat;
So oftentimes doth perfidy
Return with triple usury.

FABLE LXXIX.

THE OLD WOMAN AND HER SERVANTS.

A BELDAM kept two maids, whose spinning
    Outdid the Fates. No care had she
But setting tasks that, still beginning,
Went on to all infinity.
Phœbus had scarcely shaken out
His golden locks, ere wheels were winding,
And spindles whirled and danced about.
The spools of thread these captives binding:
Whiz—whiz; no resting; work and work!
Soon as Aurora showed her face,
A crowing Cock aroused the Turk,
Who, scrambling on her gown apace,
Lit up the lamp, and sought the bed
Where, with good will and appetite,
Each wretched servant's weary head
Had rested for the blessed night.

THE OLD WOMAN AND HER SERVANTS.

THE OLD WOMAN AND HER SERVANTS.

One opened half an eye; the other stretched
A weary arm; both, under breath,
Vowed (poor worn-out and weary wretches!)
To squeeze that Chanticleer to death.
The deed was done: they trapped the bird.
And yet it wrought them little good;
For now, ere well asleep, they heard
The old crone, fearing lest they should
O'ersleep themselves, their watchful warner gone;
She never left them less alone.

    And so it is, that often men
Who think they're getting to the shore,
Are sucked back by the sea once more.
This couple are a proof again
How near Charybdis Scylla's whirlpools roar.

FABLE LXXX.

THE ANIMALS SENDING A TRIBUTE TO ALEXANDER.

A FABLE current in the ancient times
    Had surely meaning; but none clear to me.
Its moral's somewhere, reader, in these rhymes,
So here's the thing itself for you to see.
Fame had loud rumored in a thousand places
Of Jove's great son, a certain Alexander,
Who had resolved, however sour men's faces,
To leave none free; moreover, this commander
Had summoned every living thing beneath the skies
To come and worship at his sovereign feet:
Quadrupeds, bipeds, elephants, and flies;
The bird republic, also, were to meet.
The goddess of the hundred mouths, I say,
Having thus spread a wild dismay,
By publishing the conqueror's decree,

THE ANIMALS SENDING A TRIBUTE TO ALEXANDER

The animals, and all that do obey
Their appetites alone, began to think that now
They should be kept in slavery,
And to fresh laws and other customs bow.
They meet in the wild desert and decide,
After long sittings and conflicting chatter,
To pay a tribute, pocketing their pride.
The monkey was to manage style and matter.
(Chief of all diplomats in every way);
They write down what he has to say.
The tribute only vexed the creatures:
No money! how their cash to pay?
Well, from a prince, who chanced to own
Some mines of gold they got a loan.
To bear the tribute volunteered
The Mule and Ass, and they were cheered;
The Horse and Camel lent their aid.
Then gaily started all the four,
Led by the new ambassador.
The caravan went on till, in a narrow place,
They saw his majesty the Lion's face;
They did not like his look at all,
Still less when he began to call.
"Well met; and just in time," quoth he;
"Your fellow-traveller I will be;
Your toil I wish to freely share,
My tribute's light, yet hard to bear;
I'm not accustomed to a load; so, please,
Take each a quarter at your ease,

To you 'tis nothing, that I feel;
If robbers come to pick and steal,
I shall not be the last to fight:
A Lion is not backward in a fray."
They welcome him, and he's in pleasant plight;
So, spite of Jove-sprung hero, every day
Upon the public purse he battens,
And on good deer he quickly fattens.
They reach at last a meadow land,
With flowers besprinkled, fed by brooks;
The sheep feed there on either hand,
Unguarded by the shepherd's crooks:
It is the summer zephyr's home.
No sooner has the Lion come
Than he of fever much complains;
"Continue, sirs, your embassy,"
Said he; "but burning, darting pains
Torment me now exceedingly.
I seek some herb for speedy cure;
You must not long delay, I'm sure;
Give me my money; quick! I'm hurried."
Then quickly out the gold was scurried.
The Lion, quite delighted, cried,
In tones that showed his joy and pride,
" Ye gods! my gold has hatched its brood;
And, look! the young ones are all grown
Big as the old ones; that is good:
The increase comes to me alone."
He took the whole. although he was not bid;

THE ANIMALS SENDING A TRIBUTE TO ALEXANDER.

Or if he didn't, some one like him did.
The Monkey and his retinue
Half frightened and half angry grew,
But did not dare reply; so left him there.
'Tis said that they complained at court; but where
Was then the use? in vain their loud abuse.
What could he do? Jove's royal scion!
'Twould have been Lion against Lion.
'Tis said when Corsairs fight Corsairs,
They are not minding their affairs.

FABLE LXXXI.

THE HORSE WISHING TO BE REVENGED ON THE STAG.

HORSES were once as free as air,
When man on acorns lived content.
Ass, horse, and mule unfettered went
Through field and forest, anywhere,
Without a thought of toil and care.
Nor saw one then, as in this age,
Saddles and pillions every stage,
Harness for march, and work, and battle,
Or chaises drawn by hungry cattle.
Nor were there then so many marriages,
Nor feasts that need a host of carriages.
'Twas at this time there was a keen dispute
Between a Stag who quarrelled with a Horse,
Unable to run down the nimble brute:
To kindly Man he came, for aid, of course;

THE HORSE AND THE STAG.

Man bridled him and leaped upon his back,
Nor rested till the Stag was caught and slain.
The Horse thanked heartily the Man, good lack:
"Adieu, yours truly, I'll trot off again,
Home to the wild wood and the breezy plain."
"Not quite so fast," the smiling Man replied,
"I know too well your use, you must remain;
I'll treat you well, yes, very well," he cried:
"Up to your ears the provender shall be,
And you shall feed in ease and luxury."
Alas! what's food without one's liberty?
The Horse his folly soon perceived;
But far too late the creature grieved.
His stable was all ready near the spot,
And there, with halter round his neck, he died;
Wiser had he his injuries forgot.
    Revenge is sweet to injured pride;
But it is bought too dear if bought
With that without which all things else are nought

FABLE LXXXII.

THE FOX AND THE BUST.

THE great too often wear the actor's mask;
    The vulgar worshippers the show beguiles;
The ass looks on the surface; 'tis the task
Of the wise Fox to go far deeper; full of wiles,
He pries on every side, and turns, and peeps,
And watches—Reynard never sleeps.
And when he finds in many a place
The great man nothing but a pompous face,
Repeats, what once he subtly said
Unto a hero's plaster head—
A hollow bust, and of enormous size—
Praising it with contemptuous eyes,
"Fine head," said he, "but without brains."
The saying's worth the listener's pains;
To many a noble lord the *mot* applies.

THE HORSE AND THE WOLF.

FABLE LXXXIII.

THE HORSE AND THE WOLF.

A CERTAIN Wolf, in that soft, pleasant season,
    When gentle zephyrs freshen every flower,
And animals leave home, for this good reason—
They want to make their hay before the shower:
A wolf, I say, after rough winter's rigor,
Perceived a Horse newly turned out to grass.
You may imagine what his joy was.   Vigor
Came to him when he saw the creature pass.
"Good game!" he said; "I wonder for whose spit?
No sheep this time—I only wish you were.
But this wants cunning, and some little wit:
Then let's be cunning."   So—with learned air,
As practised scholar of Hippocrates,
Who knew the virtues and demerits, too,
Of all the simples of the fields and leas,
And knew the way to cure (the praise is due)

All sorts of sad diseases—if Sir Horse
Would tell his malady, he'd cure the ill
Quite gratis; for to see him course,
Wandering untethered, at his own free will,
Showed something wrong, if science did not err.
"I have an aposthume," the Horse replied,
"Under my foot." "My son," the doctor cried,
"There is no part so sensitive to blows.
I have the honor to attend your race,
And am a surgeon, too, the whole world knows."
The rascal only waited opportunity
To leap upon the invalid's sunk flanks.
The Horse, who had mistrust, impatiently
Gave him a kick, expressive of his thanks,
That made a marmalade of teeth and jaws.
"Well done!" the Wolf growled, to himself reflecting;
"Each one should stick to his own trade. My claws
Were made for butchery, not herb-collecting."

FABLE LXXXIV.

THE SAYING OF SOCRATES.

A HOUSE was built by Socrates,
    That failed the public taste to please.
One thought the inside, not to tell a lie,
Unworthy of the wise man's dignity.
Another blamed the front; and one and all
Agreed the rooms were very much too small.
"What! such a house for our great sage,
The pride and wonder of the age!"
"Would Heaven," said he, quite weary of the Babel,
    "Were only able,
Small as it is, to fill it with true friends."
And here the story ends.

Just reason had good Socrates
To find his house too large for these.

Each man you meet as friend, your hand will claim,
Fool, if you trust the proffers that such bring.
There's nothing commoner than Friendship's name;
There's nothing rarer than the thing.

FABLE LXXXV.

THE OLD MAN AND HIS CHILDREN.

ALL power is feeble if it's disunited:
 Upon this head now hear the Phrygian slave.
If I add verse to his, which has delighted,
It's not from envy; but in hopes to grave
And paint our modern manners—feeble-sighted—
Had I ambition for mere foolish aims.
Phædrus, in eager search for glory,
Enriched full many an ancient story;
Ill-fitting me were such pretentious claims.
But let us to our fable—rather history,
Of him who tried to make his sons agree.
An Old Man, when Death called, prepared to go—
"My children dear," he said, "try now to break
This knotted sheaf of arrows. I will show
The way they're tied—what progress can you make?"
The eldest, having done his very best,

Exclaimed, "I yield them to a stronger one."
The second strove across his knee and chest,
Then passed them quickly to the younger son:
They lost their time; the bundle was too strong;
The shafts together none could snap or bend.
"Weak creatures!" said their sire, "pass them along;
My single arm the riddle soon will end."
They laughed, and thought him joking, but not so;
Singly the arrows quickly fell in twain;
"Thus may you concord's power, my children, know;
Agree in love and never part again."
He spoke no more; he felt his life was done;
And then, perceiving death was very near,
"Dear sons," said he, "I go where all have gone;
Promise to live like brothers: let me hear
Your joint vow—now, grant your father this:"
Then, weeping, each one gives the parting kiss.
He joins their hands and dies; a large estate
He left, but tangled up with heavy debts.
This creditor seized land still in debate;
That neighbor brought an action for assets:
The brothers' love was short, you well may guess;
Blood joined and interest severed the brief tie;
Ambition, envy, led to base *finesse*—
The subdivision bred chicanery.
The judge by turns condemns them all,
Neighbors and creditors assail;
To loggerheads the plighted brothers fall.
The union's sundered—one agrees

THE OLD MAN AND HIS CHILDREN.

To compromise; the other ventures on,
And soon the money is all gone
In wrangling about lawyers' fees.
They lose their wealth, and then, downhearted,
Regretful talk of how, in joke,
      Their father broke
Those arrows, when they once were parted.

FABLE LXXXVI.

THE ORACLE AND THE IMPIOUS MAN.

NONE wish to cozen heaven but the fool;
  The mystic labyrinths of the human heart
Lie open to the gods in every part:
All that man does is under their wise rule,
Even things done in darkness are revealed
To those from whom no single act's concealed.
A Pagan—a vile rogue in grain,
Whose faith in gods, it's very plain,
Was but to use them as a dictionary,
For consultation wary—
Went once to try Apollo to deceive,
With or without his leave.
"Is what I hold," he said, "alive or no?"
He held a sparrow, you must know,
Prepared to kill it or to let it fly;
To give the god at once the lie.

THE ORACLE AND THE IMPIOUS MAN.

Apollo saw the plan within his head,
      And answered—
"Dead or alive," he said, "produce your sparrow.
Try no more tricks, for I can always foil;
Such stratagems, you see, do but recoil.
I see afar, and far I cast my arrow."

FABLE LXXXVII.

THE MOUNTAIN IN LABOR.

A MOUNTAIN in labor announced the new birth
   With clamor so loud that the people all thought
'Twould at least bear a city, the largest on earth.
It was merely a Mouse that the incident brought.

When I think of this fable, so false in its fact,
And so true in its moral, it brings to my mind
Those commonplace authors who try to attract
Attention by means of the subjects they find.
"I will sing about Jove and the Titans," cries one;
But how often the song comes to nothing, when done!

FABLE LXXXVIII.

FORTUNE AND THE LITTLE CHILD.

BESIDE a well, uncurbed and deep,
    A schoolboy laid him down to sleep:
(Such rogues can do so any where.)
If some kind man had seen him there,
He would have leaped as if distracted;
But Fortune much more wisely acted;
For, passing by, she softly waked the child,
Thus whispering in accents mild:—
    I save your life, my little dear,
    And beg you not to venture here
    Again, for, had you fallen in,
    I should have had to bear the sin;
    But I demand, in reason's name,
    If for your rashness I'm to blame.
With this the goddess went her way.

I like her logic, I must say.
There takes place nothing on this planet
But Fortune ends, whoe'er began it.
In all adventures, good or ill,
We look to her to foot the bill.
Has one a stupid, empty pate,
That serves him never till too late?
He clears himself by blaming Fate.

FORTUNE AND THE LITTLE CHILD.

FABLE LXXXIX.

THE EARTHEN POT AND THE IRON POT.

"NEIGHBOR," said the iron Pot,
    "Let us go abroad a little."
"Thank you, I would rather not,"
Was the answer that he got.
    Earthenware, you know, is brittle;
And the weaker Pot was wiser
Than to trust his bad adviser.

"Mighty well for *you*," said he;
    "Skin like yours can hardly suffer
Very much by land or sea,
That is clear; but, as for *me*,
    Stop till I'm a little tougher.
You may roam the wide world over;
I shall stay at home in clover."

"Friend!" the Iron Pot replied,
    "Don't let such a fear affect you;

I shall travel at your side:
So, whatever may betide,
    Cling to me, and I'll protect you."
Having won his friend's compliance,
Off they started in alliance.

Jigging, jogging, on they went,
    Knocking one against the other
Till the Earthen Pot was sent
(Past the powers of cement)
    Into atoms by his brother.
'Twas his *own* imprudence, clearly,
That was paid for very dearly.

With our equals let us mate,
Or dread the weaker vessel's fate.

FABLE XC.

THE HARE'S EARS.

THE Lion, wounded by some subject's horn,
    Was naturally wroth, and made decree
That all by whom such ornaments were worn
From his domains forthwith should banished be.
Bulls, Rams, and Goats at once obeyed the law:
The Deer took flight, without an hour's delay.
A timid Hare felt smitten, when he saw
The shadow of his ears, with deep dismay.
He feared that somebody, with eyes too keen,
Might call them horns, they looked so very long.
"Adieu, friend Cricket," whispered he; "I mean
To quit the place directly, right or wrong.
These ears are perilous; and, though I wore
A couple short as any Ostrich wears,
I still should run." The Cricket asked, "What for?
Such ears are only natural in Hares."

"They'll pass for horns," his frightened friend replied;
"For Unicorn's appendages, I'm sure.
And folks, if I deny it, will decide
On sending me to Bedlam, as a cure."

FABLE XCI.

THE FOX WITH HIS TAIL CUT OFF.

A SLY old Fox, a foe of Geese and Rabbits,
    Was taken captive in a trap one day
(Just recompense of predatory habits),
And lost his tail before he got away.
He felt ashamed at such a mutilation;
But, cunning as before, proposed a way
To gain companions in his degradation,
And spoke as follows, on a council-day:—
"Dear brother Foxes, what can be the beauty
Or use of things so cumbrous and absurd?
They only sweep the mud up. It's your duty
To cut them off—it is, upon my word!"
"Not bad advice: there *may* be wisdom in it,"
Remarked a sage, "but will you, by-the-by,
Oblige us all by turning round a minute,
Before we give a positive reply?"

You never heard such hurricanes of laughter
As hailed the cropped appearance of the rogue
Of course, among the Foxes, ever after,
Long tails continued very much in vogue.

FABLE XCII.

THE SATYR AND THE PASSER-BY.

A SAVAGE Satyr and his brood
   Once took their lodgings and their food
Within a cavern deep and drear,
Which only very few came near.

The Satyr, with his sons and wife,
Led quite an unpretending life:
Good appetite supplies the place
Of luxuries in such a case.

A Traveller, who passed that way,
Entered the cave one rainy day;
The Satyr proved a friend in need,
By asking him to stop and feed.

The other, as 'twas pouring still,
Of course, accepted with a will;

And warmed his fingers with his breath,
For he was frozen half to death:

Upon the soup then breathed a bit
(The surest way of cooling it);
Meanwhile, his host in wonder sat,
And asked, "Pray, what's the good of that?"

"Breath cools my soup," his guest replied,
"And makes my fingers warm beside."
The Satyr answered, with a sneer,
"Then, we can do without you here.

"Beneath my roof you shall not sleep;
I scorn such company to keep.
All people in contempt I hold
Who first blow hot and then blow cold!"

THE DOCTORS.

FABLE XCIII.

THE DOCTORS.

ONE morning Doctor Much-the-Worse went out
    To see a patient, who was also tended
By Doctor Much-the-Better. "Past a doubt,"
The former said, "this case is nearly ended.
There's not a chance."—The latter trusted still
In physic's aid: but while the twin concocters
Disputed hard on plaster, draught, and pill,
The patient died from this attack of doctors.
"Look there," said one, "I told you how 'twould be!"
The other said, "No doubt you're vastly clever;
But if our friend had only followed *me*,
I know he would have been as well as ever."

FABLE XCIV.

THE LABORING MAN AND HIS CHILDREN.

W ORK, work, with all your might and main,
    For labor brings the truest gain.

A wealthy Laborer lay near to death;
And, summoning his children round the bed,
He thus addressed them, with his latest breath:
"Part not with my estate when I am dead.
My parents left me what I leave to *you*.
About the place a treasure lies concealed,
No matter where,—search every corner through,
Nor leave a spot unturned in any field.
Go, seek it from the morning till the night."
Their father dead, the loving sons fulfilled
The dying wish, that made their labor light:
From end to end the fields were duly tilled.
The harvest was enormous, though they found
No golden treasures, howsoever small.
And yet the father's last advice was sound,
For Labor *is* a treasure, after all.

THE HEN WITH THE GOLDEN EGGS.

FABLE XCV.

THE HEN WITH THE GOLDEN EGGS.

MY little story will explain
    An olden maxim, which expresses
How Avarice, in search of gain,
May lose the hoard that it possesses.
The fable tells us that a Hen
Laid golden eggs, each egg a treasure;
Its owner—stupidest of men—
Was miserly beyond all measure.
He thought a mine of wealth to find
Within the Hen, and so he slew it:
He found a bird of common kind—
And lost a pretty fortune through it.

For money-worms, who now and then
Grow poor through trying to be wealthy,
I tell my fable of the Hen;
My tale is good, my moral healthy.

FABLE XCVI.

THE ASS THAT CARRIED THE RELICS.

AN Ass, with relics loaded, thought the crowd
    Knelt down to him, and straightway grew so proud;
He took to his own merit, without qualms,
Even the incense and loud chanted psalms.
Some one, to undeceive him, wisely said—
"A foolish vanity has turned your head:
They not to you, but to the idol, pray;
Where glory's due, there they the honor pay."

When foolish magistrates rule o'er a town,
It's not the man we bow to, but his gown.

FABLE XCVII.

THE SERPENT AND THE FILE.

A SERPENT once and Watchmaker were neighbors
(Unpleasant neighbor for a working man):
The Snake came creeping in among his labors,
Seeking for food on the felonious plan;
But all the broth he found was but a File,
And that he gnawed in vain—the steel was tough.
The tool said, with a calm, contemptuous smile,
"Poor and mistaken thing! that's *quantum suff*.
You lose your time, you shallow sneak, you do;
You'll never bite a farthing's worth off me,
Though you break all your teeth: I tell you true,
I fear alone Time's great voracity."

This is for critics—all the baser herd,
Who, restless, gnaw at everything they find.

Bah! you waste time, you do, upon my word;
Don't think your teeth can pierce the thinnest rind:
To injure noble works you try, and try, but can't;
To you they're diamond, steel, and adamant.

FABLE XCVIII.

THE HARE AND THE PARTRIDGE.

ONE should not mock the wretched.   Who can tell
    He will be always happy?   Fortune changes.
Wise Æsop, in his fables, taught this well.
My story is like his—which very strange is.
The Hare and Partridge shared the selfsame clover,
And lived in peace and great tranquillity,
Till one day, racing all the meadows over,
The huntsmen came and forced the Hare to flee,
And seek his hiding-place.   The dogs, put out,
Were all astray: yes, even Brifaut erred,
Until the scent betrayed.   A lusty shout
Arouses Miraut, who then loud averred,
From philosophic reasoning, 'twas the Hare,
And ardently pushed forward the pursuit.
Rustaut, who never lied, saw clearly where
Had homeward turned the frightened brute.

Poor wretch! it came to its old form to die.
The cruel Partridge, bitter taunting, said,
"You boasted of your fleetness; now, then, try
Your nimble feet."   Soon was that scorn repaid:
While she still laughed, the recompense was near.
She thought her wings would save her from man's jaws.
Poor creature! there was worse than that to fear:
The swooping Goshawk came with cruel claws.

THE STAG AND THE VINE.

FABLE XCIX.

THE STAG AND THE VINE.

A STAG behind a lofty Vine took shelter
  (Such vines are met with in a southern clime);
Hunters and hounds pursued him helter-skelter,
And searched and searched, but only lost their time.
The huntsmen laid, as might have been expected,
Upon the shoulders of their dogs the blame.
The Stag, forgetting he had been protected,
Vastly ungrateful all at once became;
Upon the friendly Vine he made a dinner;
But hounds and hunters soon came back again.
Discovered quickly—now the leaves were thinner—
The Stag, of course, got set upon and slain.
"I merit this!" exclaimed the dying glutton;
"Ingratitude, like pride, must have a fall:"
Another gasp, and he was dead as mutton;
And no one present pitied him at all.

How oft is hospitality rewarded
By deeds ungrateful as the one recorded!

FABLE C.

THE LION GOING TO WAR.

THE Lion planned a foray on a foe;
    Held a war-council; sent his heralds out
To warn the Animals he'd strike a blow;
Soon all were ready to help slay and rout—
Each in his special way.   The Elephant,
To bear upon his back the baggage and supplies,
And fight, as usual.   Then the Bear, to plant
The flag upon the breach.   The Fox's eyes
Brighten at thought of diplomatic guile.
The Monkey hopes to dupe with endless tricks.
"But send away the Asses," says, meanwhile,
Some courtier, in whose mind the fancy sticks;
"They're only stupid.   Pack off, too, the Hares."
"No, not so," said the King; "I'll use them all:
Our troop's imperfect, if they have no shares.
The Ass shall be our startling trumpet call;

THE LION GOING TO WAR.

The Hare is useful for our courier, mind."
Prudent and wise the King who knows the way
For every subject fitting task to find.
Nothing is useless to the wise, they say.

FABLE CI.

THE ASS IN THE LION'S SKIN.

A DONKEY donned a Lion's hide,
And spread a panic far and wide
(Although the Donkey, as a rule,
Is not a fighter, but a fool).
By chance, a little bit of ear
Stuck forth, and made the matter clear.
Then Hodge, not relishing the trick,
Paid off its author with a stick.
While those who saw the Lion's skin,
But little dreamed who lurked within,
Stood open-mouthed, and all aghast,
To see a Lion run so fast.

This tale applies, unless I err,
To many folks who make a stir,
And owe three-fourths of their success
To servants, carriages, and dress.

THE EAGLE AND THE OWL.

FABLE CII.

THE EAGLE AND THE OWL.

THE Eagle and the Owl had treaty made—
　Ceased quarrelling, and even had embraced.
One took his royal oath; and, undismayed,
The other's claw upon his heart was placed:
Neither would gulp a fledgling of the other.
"Do you know mine?" Minerva's wise bird said.
The Eagle gravely shook his stately head.
"So much the worse," the Owl replied. "A mother
Trembles for her sweet chicks—she does, indeed.
It's ten to one if I can rear them then.
You are a king, and, therefore, take no heed
Of who or what. The gods and lords of men
Put all things on one level: let who will
Say what they like. Adieu, my children dear,
If you once meet them." "Nay, good ma'am, but still,
Describe them," said the Eagle; "have no fear:

LA FONTAINE'S FABLES.

Be sure I will not touch them, on my word."
The Owl replied. "My little ones are small,
Beautiful, shapely,—prettier, far, than all.
By my description you will know the dears;
Do not forget it; let no fate by you
Find way to us, and cause me ceaseless tears."
Well, one fine evening, the old Owl away,
The Eagle saw, upon a rocky shelf,
Or in a ruin, (who cares which I say?)
Some little ugly creatures.   To himself
The Eagle reasoned, "These are not our friend's,
Moping and gruff, and such a screeching, too:
Let's eat 'em."   Waste time never spends
The royal bird, to give the brute his due;
And when he eats, he eats, to tell the truth.
The Owl, returning only found the feet
Of her dear offspring:—sad, but yet it's sooth,
She mourns the children, young, and dear, and sweet,
And prays the gods to smite the wicked thief,
That brought her all the woe and misery.
Then some one said, "Restrain thy unjust grief;
Reflect one moment on the casualty.
Thou art to blame, and also Nature's law,
Which makes us always think our own the best.
You sketched them to the Eagle as you saw:
They were not like your portrait; am I just?"

FABLE CIII.

THE SHEPHERD AND THE LION.

FABLES are sometimes more than they appear:
    A crude, bare moral wearies some, I fear.
The simplest animal to truth may lead;
The story and the precept make one heed:
They pass together better than apart:
To please and yet instruct, that is the art.
To write for writing's sake seems poor to me;
And for this reason, more especially—
Numbers of famous men, from time to time,
Have written fables in laconic rhyme,
Shunning all ornament and verbose length,
Wasting no word, unless to gain in strength
Phædrus was so succinct, some men found fault;
Curt Æsop was far readier still to halt.
But, above all, a Greek* did most excel,
Who in four verses told what he would tell.

        * Gabrias.

If he succeeded, let the experts say;
Let's match him now with Æsop, by the way.
A Shepherd and a Hunter they will bring:
I give the point and ending as they sing,
Embroidering here and there, as on I go;—
Thus Æsop told the story, you must know.

A Shepherd, finding in his flocks some gaps,
Thought he might catch the robber in his traps,
And round a cave drew close his netted toils,
Fearing the Wolves, and their unceasing spoils.
"Grant, king of gods, before I leave the place,"
He cried, "grant me to see the brigand's face.
Let me but watch him rolling in the net,
That is the dearest pleasure I could get!"
Then from a score of calves he chose the beast,
The fattest, for the sacrificial feast.
That moment stepped a Lion from the cave;
The Shepherd, prostrate, all intent to save
His petty life, exclaimed, "How little we
Know what we ask! If I could only see
Safe in my snares, that caused me so much grief,
The helpless, panting, miserable thief,
Great Jove! a Calf I promised to thy fane:
An Ox I'd make it, were I free again."

Thus wrote our leading author of his race;
Now for the imitator in his place.

FABLE CIV.

THE LION AND THE HUNTER.

A BRAGGART, lover of the chase,
    Losing a dog of noble race,
Fearing 'twas in a Lion's maw,
Asked the first shepherd that he saw
If he would kindly show him where
The robber had his favorite lair;
That he might teach him, at first sight,
The difference between wrong and right.
The shepherd said, "Near yonder peak
You'll find the gentleman you seek.
A sheep a month, that is the fee
I pay for ease and liberty.
I wander where I like, you see.
And, while he spoke, the Lion ran
And put to flight the bragging man.
"O Jupiter!" he cried, "befriend,
And some safe refuge quickly send!"

LA FONTAINE'S FABLES.

The proof of courage, understand,
Is shown when danger is at hand.
Some, when the danger comes, 'tis known,
Will very quickly change their tone.

FABLE CV.

PHŒBUS AND BOREAS.

PHŒBUS and Boreas saw a traveller,
   'Fended against bad weather prudently.
Autumn had just begun, and then, you see,
Caution is useful to the wayfarer.
It rains and shines, and rainbows bright displayed
Warned those who ventured out to take a cloak:
The Romans called these months, as if in joke,
The doubtful. For this season well arrayed,
Our fellow, ready for the pelting rain,
Wore a cloak doubled, and of sturdy stuff.
" He thinks," the Wind said, "he is armed enough
To 'scape all hazards; but it's quite in vain,
For he has not foreseen that I can blow,
So that no button in the world avails:
I send cloaks flying as I do ships' sails.
It will amuse us just to let him know;

Now, you shall see." "Agreed," then Phœbus said:
"Then let us bet, without more talking, come,
Which of us first shall send him cloakless home:
You can begin, and I will hide my head."
'Twas soon arranged, and Boreas filled his throat
With vapor, till his cheeks balloons became.
A demon's holiday of lightning-flame
And storm came whistling, wrecking many a boat,
Shattering many a roof—and all for what?
About a paltry cloak. He's much ado
To save him from a precipice or two.
The Wind but wasted time—one's pleased at that—
The more it raged, but firmer still he drew
Around his breast the cloak: the cape just shook,
And here and there a shred the tempest took.
At last the time was up, no more it blew,
Then the hot Sun dispersed the cloudy haze,
And pierced the weary horseman through and through.
Beneath his heavy mantle sprung hot dew—
No longer could he bear those fervent rays—
He threw his cloak aside (a man of sense);
Not half his power had Phœbus yet employed.
Mildness had won—the Sun was overjoyed:
Softness gains more than any violence.

THE BEAR AND THE TWO FRIENDS.

FABLE CVI.

THE BEAR AND THE TWO FRIENDS.

TWO Friends, in want, resolved to sell
    A Bear-skin, though the Bear was well,
And still alive. The Furrier paid
Them willingly; the bargain's made.
It was the King of Bears, they said:
They'd kill him in an hour or two,
And what more could they hope to do?
"The merchant has not such a skin,
A guarantee, through thick and thin,
To fence from e'en the keenest cold
With warm, soft, pliant fold on fold:
Better to make two cloaks than one."
The bargain's made, the business done,
The Bear, in two days, was to die:
That they agreed on presently.
They found the Bear, who, at full trot,

Came down upon them, raging hot.
The men were thunder-struck; soon done
With bargain-making, how they run!
Life against money: they are mute.
One climbs a tree, to shun the brute;
The other, cold as marble, lies
Upon his stomach—shuts his eyes;
For he has heard that Bears, instead
Of eating, fear to touch the dead.
The trap deceives the foolish Bear:
He sees the body lying there,
Suspects a trick, turns, smells and sniffs,
With many nuzzling, cautious whiffs.
"He's dead," said he, "and rather high;"
Then seeks the forest that's hard by.
The merchant, from the tree descending
Quickly, to his companion's lending
The aid he needs. "A wondrous sight,
To think you've only had a fright.
But where's his skin?—and did he say
Aught in your ear, as there you lay?
For he came, as I plainly saw,
And turned you over with his paw."
"He said, 'Another time, at least,
Before you sell, first kill the beast.'"

FABLE CVII.

JUPITER AND THE FARMER.

JUPITER had a farm to give away;
    Mercury told the world the chosen day.
The people came to offer; rough they were,
And listened grimly. One said it was bare
And stubborn land; another half agreed.
While they thus haggled, churlishly indeed,
One bolder than the rest—but wiser?—no—
Consents to take it, if Jove only grant
The climate that he wishes; he will plant,
And sow, and reap, if but the heat and cold
May come and go, like slaves, as they are told—
The seasons wait his nod: the wet and dry
Obey his bidding from a servile sky.
Jove grants his wish—our foolish fellow sways
His sceptre bravely—rains and blows for days;
Makes his own climate just as he may please

His neighbors, no more than Antipodes,
Share his good weather.   Still as well they fare;
Their barns are teeming full; but his are bare.
The next year quite a change; another way
He sets the seasons, watching day by day:
Still, there's some flaw—his crops are thin and poor,
While loaded waggons crowd his neighbor's door.
What can he do?—he falls before Jove's throne,
Confesses all his folly: he alone
Has been to blame.   Jove, with much gentleness,
Like a mild master, pities his distress.
It is agreed that Providence is kind,
And knows far better than a human mind
What's good for us, and calmly bids us do it:
We seldom see our way till we are through it.

THE STAG VIEWING HIMSELF IN THE STREAM.

FABLE CVIII.

THE STAG VIEWING HIMSELF IN THE STREAM

BESIDE a fountain in the wood
    A royal Stag admiring stood:
  His antlers pleased him well.
But one thing vexed him to the heart:
His slender legs ill matched the part
  On which he loved to dwell.

"Nature has shaped them ill," said he,
Watching their shadows peevishly:
  "Here is a disproportion!
My horns rise branching, tall, and proud;
My legs disgrace them, 'tis allowed,
  And are but an abortion."

Just then a deer-hound frightened him,
And lent a wing to every limb.
  O'er bush and brake—he's off!

At those adornments on his brow
The foolish creature praised just now
   He soon begins to scoff.

Upon his legs his life depends:
They are his best and only friends.
   He unsays every word,
And curses Heaven, that has sent
A dangerous gift. We all repent
   Speeches that are absurd.

We prize too much the beautiful,
And useful things spurn (as a rule);
   Yet fast will beauty fleet.
The Stag admired the antlers high,
That brought him into jeopardy,
   And blamed his kindly feet.

FABLE CIX.

THE COCKEREL, THE CAT, AND THE LITTLE RAT.

A RAT, so very young that it had seen
    Nothing at all, was at his setting out
Almost snapped up; and what his fears had been
He told his mother.   Thus it came about—
" I crossed the mountains bordering our land,
 Bold as a Rat that has his way to make,
When two great animals, you understand,
Before my eyes their way towards me take.
The one was gentle, tender, and so mild;
The other restless, wild and turbulent;
A screeching voice, some flesh upon its head,
A sort of arm raised as for punishment.
His tail a plume, a fiery plume displayed
(It was a capon that the creature drew
Like a wild beast new come from Africa);
And with his arms he beat his sides, it's true,

With such a frightful noise that, in dismay,
E'en I, who pride myself on courage, ran
And fled for fear, cursing the evil creature;
As, but for him, I should have found a plan
To make acquaintance with that gentle nature—
So soft and sweet, and with a skin like ours;
Long tail, and spotted, with a face so meek;
And yet a glittering eye, of such strange powers:
A sympathizer, sure as I can speak,
With us the Rats, for he has just such ears.
I was about to make a little speech,
When, all at once, as if to rouse my fears,
The other creature gave a dreadful screech,
And I took flight." "My child," exclaimed the Rat,
"That gentle hypocrite you liked so well
Was our malignant enemy—the Cat.
The other, on whose form so foul you fell,
Is simply harmless, and will be our meal,
Perhaps, some day; while, as for that meek beast,
On us he dearly loves to leap and steal,
And crunch and munch us for his cruel feast.
Take care, my child, in any case,
Judge no one by their look or face."

FABLE CX.

THE FOX, THE MONKEY, AND THE OTHER ANIMALS

THE Animals (the Lion dead)
Resolved to choose a King instead;
The crown was taken from its case—
A dragon guarded well the place.
They tried the crown, but when they'd done,
It would not fit a single one.
Some heads too large, and some too small;
Many had horns,—defects in all.
The Monkey, laughing, tried it, too,
And got his mocking visage through,
With many wild, fantastic faces;
And twisting gambols and grimaces.
A hoop, at last, around his waist
He wore it, and they cried, "Well placed!"
He was elected. Each one paid
Their homage to the King they'd made.

The Fox alone laments the choice,
But chokes it down with flattering voice.
Paying his little compliments,
To hide his secret sentiments.
"Sire," to the King, he said, "I've pleasure
To tell you I have found a treasure;
A secret, but to me alone—
All treasures fall unto the throne."
The young King, eager at finance,
Ran fast himself, to catch the chance.
It was a trap, and he was caught.
The Fox said, when his aid he sought,
"You think to govern us and rule;
You cannot save yourself, you fool!"
They turned him out, and, with some wit,
Agreed that few a crown will fit.

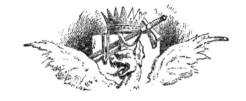

FABLE CXI.

THE MULE THAT BOASTED OF HIS FAMILY.

AN Episcopal Mule, of its family proud,
    Would *not* keep his ancestry under a cloud,
But chattered, and bragged of his mother the mare:
Of her having done this, and her having been there;
And vowed that so famous a creature ignored,
Was a shame and disgrace to historian's record.
He frankly disdained on a doctor to wait,
And patiently stand at a poor patient's gate.
At last, growing old, in the mill he's confined,
Then his father, the donkey, came into his mind.

A misfortune is useful, if only to bring
A fool to his senses—a very good thing—
It's sent for a purpose, and always will be
Useful to some one or something, you see.

FABLE CXII.

THE OLD MAN AND THE ASS.

AN Old Man, riding on a Donkey, saw
    A meadow thick with flowers, and full of grass.
He instantly unbridled the poor Ass,
And let him roam for twenty minutes' law.
It scratch'd, and scratch'd, and munch'd, and chew'd, and bray'd
Nipping the best, and kicking, for sheer fun:
The meal refreshing was betimes begun.
Just then the enemy came, all arrayed;
"Fly," said the Old Man. "Wherefore?" said the beast:
"Am I to carry double burden—double load?
Am I to tramp once more upon the road?"
"No," said the Old Man; "I'll stop here, at least."
"To whom I may belong is no great matter.
Go, save yourself from an unlucky blow;
My master is my enemy, I know:
I tell you in the best French I can patter."

THE COUNTRYMAN AND THE SERPENT.

FABLE CXIII.

THE COUNTRYMAN AND THE SERPENT.

ÆSOP describes, as he's well able,
    A Peasant, wise and charitable,
Who, walking on a winter day
Around his farm, found by the way
A snake extended on the snow,
Frozen and numb—half-dead, you know.
He lifts the beast, with friendly care,
And takes him home to warmer air—
Not thinking what reward would be
Of such an unwise charity.
Beside the hearth he stretches him,
Warms and revives each frozen limb.
The creature scarcely feels the glow,
Before its rage begins to flow:
First gently raised its head and rolled
Its swelling body, fold on fold;

Then tried to leap, and spring, and bite
Its benefactor;—was that right?
"Ungrateful!" cried the man; "then I
Will give you now your due—you die!"
With righteous anger came the blow
From the good axe. It struck, and, lo!
Two strokes—three snakes—its body, tail,
And head; and each, without avail,
Trying to re-unite in vain—
They only wriggle in long pain.

It's good to lavish charity;
But then, on whom? Well, that's just it.
As for ungrateful men, they die
In misery, and as 'tis fit.

FABLE CXIV.

THE HARE AND THE TORTOISE.

IT'S not enough that you run fleet;
    Start early,—that's the way to beat.

The Tortoise said unto the Hare,
"I'll bet you, free, and frank, and fair,
You do not reach a certain place
So soon as I, though quick your pace."
"So soon?" the nimble creature cries;
"Take physic for your brains;—be wise"—
"Fool or no fool, I make the bet."
The bet is made, the stakes are set;
But who the sporting judges were
Is neither your nor my affair.
Our Hare had but a bound to make,
From him the swiftest hounds to shake.
They run themselves almost to death,

Yet he is scarcely out of breath;
Plenty of time for him to browse,
To sleep, and then again to rouse;
Or boldly turn the while he's going,
And mark which way the wind is blowing.
Careless, he lets the Tortoise pace,
Grave as a senator.   To race
With such a thing is but disgrace.
She, in the meanwhile, strives and strains,
And takes most meritorious pains;
Slow, yet unceasing.   Still the Hare
Holds it a very mean affair
To start too soon; but when, at last,
The winning-post is almost past
By his dull rival, then, 'tis true
He quicker than the arrow flew.
Alas! his efforts failed to win,
The Tortoise came the first one in.
"Well," she said then, "now, was I right?
What use was all your swiftness: light
I held your speed, and won the prize;
Where would you be, can you surmise,
If with my house upon your shoulders
You tried to startle all beholders?"

THE SICK LION AND THE FOX.

FABLE CXV.

THE SICK LION AND THE FOX.

THE King of Beasts was sick to death,
    And, almost with his latest breath,
Made known to all his vassals he
Needed their deepest sympathy.
As in his cave he lay, he stated
For friendly visitors he waited.
With every guarantee insured,
The deputies went, quite secured;
Upon the Lion's passport writ,
In fair round hand, each word of it—
A promise good, in eyes of law,
Whether against tooth or claw.
The Prince's will to execute
Goes every class of beast and brute.
The Foxes only kept at home;
One gave the reason he'd not come:

LA FONTAINE'S FABLES.

"The footprints of the courtiers, see,
Are all one way, that's plain to me:
But none point homeward. It is just
If I feel somewhat of distrust.
Our sick King's courtiers may dispense
With passports, for they're full of sense.
Granted, no doubt; and yet I crave
They'll show me how to leave the cave
I clearly see they enter. Well!
But how they leave it who can tell?"

FABLE CXVI.

THE ASS AND HIS MASTERS.

A GARDENER'S Donkey once complained to Fate
Of having to rise earlier than the sun.
"The cocks," he said, "are certainly not late;
But I have got to rise ere they've begun.
And all for what?—to carry herbs to sell:
A pretty cause to break one's morning sleep!"
Fate, touched by this appeal, determined well
To give the beast to other hands to keep:
The Gardener to a Tanner yields him next.
The weight of hides, and their distressing fume,
Soon shock our friend; he is far worse perplexed;
His mind again begins to lower and gloom.
"I much regret," he said, "my first good man,
For when he turned his head I always got
A bite of cabbage;—that was just my plan:
It cost me not a single sous, or jot;

But here no, no rewards but kick and cuff."—
His fortune shifts; a Charcoal-dealer's stall
Receives him.   Still complaints, and *quantum suff*.
"What! not content yet," Fate cries, "after all?
This Ass is worse than half a hundred kings.
Does he, forsooth, think he's the only one
That's not content?   Have I no other things
To fill my mind but this poor simpleton?"
And Fate was right.   No man is satisfied:
Our fortune never fits our wayward minds;
The present seems the worst we've ever tried;
We weary Heaven with outcries of all kinds.
And yet if Jupiter gave each his will,
We should torment his ear with wishes still.

FABLE CXVII.

THE SUN AND THE FROGS.

A MONARCH'S wedding gave his people up,
    The whole day long, to dances and the cup;
But Æsop found their doings in bad taste,
And thought their joy decidely misplaced.

"The Sun," said he, "once thought about a wife,
And fancied he could shine in married life;
But instantly there came petitions loud
From all the Frogs on earth—a noisy crowd.
'Suppose,' they said, 'the Queen should be prolific,
Our situation will become terrific.
A single sun is quite enough to bear;
The little ones will drive us to despair.
Parched as we are, in sultry summer weather,
The extra heat will roast us altogether.

Let us entreat your mercy on our race;
The river Styx is not a pleasant place!'"

Considering that Frogs are very small,
I think the argument not bad at all.

THE CARTER STUCK IN THE MUD.

FABLE CXVIII.

THE CARTER STUCK IN THE MUD.

A PHAETON, who drove a load of hay,
    Found himself in the mud stuck hard and fast:
Poor man! from all assistance far away.
(In Lower Brittany he had been cast,
Near Quimper-Corentin, and all may know
'Tis there that Destiny sends folks she hates.
God keep us from such journey here below.)
But to return. The Carter, in the mire,
Rages and swears, and foams and execrates—
His eyes wild rolling, and his face on fire;
Curses the holes, the horses, every stone,
The cart, and then himself. The god he prays,
Whose mighty labors through the world are known
"O Hercules! send present aid," he says;
"If thy broad back once bore this mighty sphere,
Thy arm can drag me out." His prayer he ends.

Then came a voice from out a cloud quite near:
"To those who strive themselves he succor lends.
Work, and find out where the obstruction lies;
Remove this bird-lime mud you curse so hot;
Clear axle-tree and wheel—be quick and wise;
Take up the pick, and break that flint—why not?
Fill up that yawning rut. Now, is it done?"
"Yes," said the man; and then the voice replied,
"Now I can help you; take your whip, my son."
"I've got it. Hallo! here; what's this?" he cried;
"My cart goes nicely—praise to Hercules."
And then the voice—"You see how readily
Your horses got clear out of jeopardy."
To those who help themselves the gods send help and ease.

FABLE CXIX.

THE DOG AND THE SHADOW.

WE all deceive ourselves, and so we fall;
    We all run after shadows, in our way:
So many madmen, one can't count them all;
Send them to Æsop's Dog,—I beg and pray.
The Dog, who saw the shadow of the meat
He carried, dark upon the liquid tide,
Dropping his prey, snapped at the counterfeit:
The river rose, and washed him from the side.
True, with much danger he regained the shore,
But neither meat nor shadow saw he more.

FABLE CXX.

THE BIRD-CATCHER, THE HAWK, AND THE SKYLARK.

INJUSTICE, and false people's wilful crimes,
  Serve others as excuses, oftentimes,
For fresh injustice. Nature's law's planned so;
If you wish to be spared, then give no blow.

A Countryman, with glittering looking-glass,
Was catching birds. The brilliant phantom lured
A Lark; when, suddenly, it came to pass
A Sparrow Hawk, of its sweet prey assured,
Dropped from the cloud, and struck swift to the ground
The gentlest bird that sings; though near the tomb,
She had escaped the trap; yet now she found
Beneath that cruel beak at last her doom.
Whilst stripping her, eager and all intent,
The Hawk itself beneath the net was caught.

THE BIRD-CATCHER, THE HAWK AND THE SKYLARK.

"Fowler," he cried, "no harm I ever meant:
I never did thee ill, nor ever sought
To do."   The man replied, "This helpless thing
Had done no more to thee;—no murmuring!"

FABLE CXXI.

THE HORSE AND THE ASS.

IN this world every one must help his brother.
    If your poor neighbor dies, his weary load
On you, perhaps, may fall, and on no other.

An Ass and Horse were travelling on the road:
The last had but the harness on his back.
The first, borne down unto the very ground,
Besought the Horse to help him, or, alack!
He'd never reach the town. In duty bound,
Apologies he made for this request:
"To you," he said, "the load would be mere sport."
The Horse refused, and snorted at the jest.
Just as he sneered, the Donkey died. In short,
He soon perceived he had not acted right,
And had his friend ill treated; for that night
They made him drag the cart through thick and thin,
And in the cart his injured comrade's skin.

FABLE CXXII.

THE CHARLATAN.

OF Charlatans the world has never lack:
    This science of professors has no want.
Only the other day one made his vaunt
He could cheat Acheron; in white and black
Another boasted o'er the town that, lo!
He was another Cicero.

One of these fellows claimed a mastery
Of eloquence; swore he could make an ass,
"A peasant, rustic, booby, d'ye see?—
Yes, gentlemen, a dolt of basest class—
Eloquent. Bring me an ass," he cried,
"The veriest ass, and I will teach him so
He shall the cassock wear with proper pride."
The Prince resolved the truth of this to know.
"I have," he to the rhetorician one day said,

LA FONTAINE'S FABLES.

"A fine ass from Arcadia in my stable;
Make him an orator if you are able."
"Sire, you do what you will." The man they made
Accept a sum, for twenty years to teach
The ass the proper use of speech;
And if he failed, he in the market-place,
With halter round his neck, was to be hung;
Upon his back his rhetoric books all strung,
And asses' ears above his frightened face.
One of the courtiers said that he would go
And see him at the gibbet; he'd such grace
And presence, he'd become the hangman's show:
There, above all, his art would come in well:
A long-extended speech—with pathos, too—
Would fit the great occasion, so it fell
In the one form of those grand Ciceros
Vulgarly known as thieves. "Yes, that is true,"
The other said; "but ere I try,
The king, the ass, and you will die."

THE YOUNG WIDOW.

FABLE CXXIII.

THE YOUNG WIDOW.

A HUSBAND isn't lost without a sigh;
   We give a groan, then are consoled again;
Swift on Time's wings we see our sorrow fly;
Fleet Time brings sunshine's pleasure after rain.
     The widow of a year, the widow of a day,
       Are very different, I say:
One finds it almost hard to trust one's eyes,
Or the same face to recognize.
One flies the world, the other plans her wiles;
In true or untrue sighs the one pours forth her heart,
Yet the same note they sing, or tears or smiles—
"Quite inconsolable," they say; but, for my part,
I don't heed that. This fable shows the truth:
Yet why say fiction?—it is sooth.

The husband of a beauty, young and gay,

Unto another world was call'd away.
"My soul, wait for me!" was the Widow's moan.
The husband waited not, but went alone.
The Widow had a father—prudent man!
He let her tears flow; 'twas the wisest plan.
Then to console, "My child," he said, "this way
Of weeping will soon wash your charms away.
There still live men: think no more of the dead:
I do not say at once I would be wed;
But after a short time you'll see, I know,
A husband young and handsome that I'll show,
By no means like the sorry one you mourn."
"A cloister is my husband—ah! forlorn."
The father lets these foolish groans go by;
A month pass'd—every moment tear or sigh.
Another month, and ribbons load her table;
She changed her dress, and cast away her sable.
The flock of Cupids to the dovecot back
Came flying, now unscared by scarecrow black;
Smiles, sports and dances follow in their train;
She bathes in youth's bright fountain once again.
No more the father fears the dear deceased;
But, as his silence not one whit decreased,
The angry widow cries impatiently,
"Where's the young husband that you promised me?"

FABLE CXXIV.

DISCORD.

DISCORD, who had the gods entangled
    About an apple—how they wrangled!—
Was driven from the skies at last,
And to that animal came fast
That they call Man; her brother, too,
"Whether or no," who long'd to view
Our ball of earth.   Her father came—
Old "Thine and Mine"—the very same.
She did much honor to our sphere
By longing so much to be here;
She cared not for the other race
Who watch us from aerial space—
We were gross folk, not tamed the least,
Who married without law or priest—
Discord no business had at all:
The proper places where to call

Scandal has orders to find out;
She, a right busy, active scout,
Falls quick to quarrel and debates,
And always Peace anticipates:
Blows up a spark into a blaze,
Not to burn out for many days.
Scandal, at length complain'd she found
No refuge certain above ground,
And often lost her precious time:
She must have shelter in this clime—
A point from whence she could send forth
Discord, west, east, or south, or north.
There were no nunneries then, you see:
That made it difficult, may be.
The inn of Wedlock was assign'd
At last, and suited Scandal's mind.

THE ANIMALS SICK OF THE PLAGUE.

FABLE CXXV.

THE ANIMALS SICK OF THE PLAGUE.

A MALADY that Heaven sent
    On earth, for our sin's punishment—
The Plague (if I must call it right),
Fit to fill Hades in a night—
Upon the animals made war;
Not all die, but all stricken are.
They scarcely care to seek for food,
For they are dying, and their brood.
The Wolves and Foxes crouching keep,
Nor care to watch for timorous Sheep.
Even the very Turtle-doves
Forget their little harmless loves.
The Lion, calling counsel, spoke—
" Dear friends, upon our luckless crown
Heaven misfortune has sent down,
For some great sin. Let, then, the worst
Of all our race be taken first,

And sacrificed to Heaven's ire;
So healing Mercury, through the fire,
May come and free us from this curse,
That's daily growing worse and worse.
History tells us, in such cases
For patriotism there a place is.
No self-deception;—plain and flat
Search each his conscience, mind you that.
I've eaten several sheep, I own.
What harm had they done me?—why, none.
Sometimes—to be quite fair and true—
I've eaten up the shepherd too.
I will devote myself; but, first,
Let's hear if any has done worse.
Each must accuse himself, as I
Have done; for justice would let die
The guiltiest one." The Fox replied—
"You are too good to thus decide.
Your Majesty's kind scruples show
Too much of delicacy. No!
What! eating sheep—the paltry—base,
Is that a sin? You did the race,
In munching them, an honor—yes,
I'm free, your highness, to confess.
And as for shepherds, they earn all
The evils that upon them fall:
Being of those who claim a sway
(Fantastic claim!) o'er us, they say."
Thus spoke the Fox the flatterer's text.

THE ANIMALS SICK OF THE PLAGUE.

The Tiger and the Bear came next,
With claims that no one thought perplexed.
In fact, more quarrelsome they were
The fewer grew the cavillers there.
Even the humblest proved a saint:
None made a slanderous complaint.
The Ass came in his turn, and said,
"For one thing I myself upbraid.
Once, in a rank green abbey field,
Sharp hunger made me basely yield.
The opportunity was there;
The grass was rich; the day was fair.
Some demon tempted me: I fell,
And cleared my bare tongue's length, pell-mell,'
Scarce had he spoken ere they rose
In arms, nor waited for the close.
A Wolf, half lawyer, made a speech,
And proved this creature wrong'd them each
And all, and they must sacrifice
This scurvy wretch, who to his eyes
Was steep'd in every wickedness.
Doom'd to the rope, without redress,
"Hang him at once! What! go and eat
An Abbot's grass, however sweet!
Abominable crime!" they cry;
"Death only clears the infamy."

If you are powerful, wrong or right,
The court will change your black to white.

FABLE CXXVI.

THE RAT WHO RETIRED FROM THE WORLD

THERE is a legend of the Levantine,
    That once a certain Rat, weary of strife,
Retired into a Dutch cheese, calm, serene,
Far from the bustle and the cares of life.
In solitude extreme, dim stretching far and wide,
The hermit dwelt in all tranquillity,
And worked so well with feet and teeth inside,
Shelter and food were his in certainty.
What need of more? Soon he grew fat with pride;
God showers his blessings upon those who pay
Their vows to him in faith. There came, one day,
A pious deputy, from Ratdom sent,
To beg some trifling alms, because their town—
Ratopolis—was leaguered with intent
Most deadly; they, without a crown,
Had been obliged to fly,—so indigent

THE RAT WHO RETIRED FROM THE WORLD.

Was the assailed republic.   Little ask
The scared ambassadors—the succor sure,
In a few days; the loan was no hard task.
" My friend," the hermit cried, " I can endure
No more the things of this world.   What have I,
A poor recluse, to give you but a prayer?
I yield you patiently unto His care."
And then he shut the door quite tranquilly.

Who do I mean, then, by this selfish Rat?
A monk?—no, sir; a dervish is more fat.
A monk, where'er in this world he may be,
Is always full, you know, of charity.

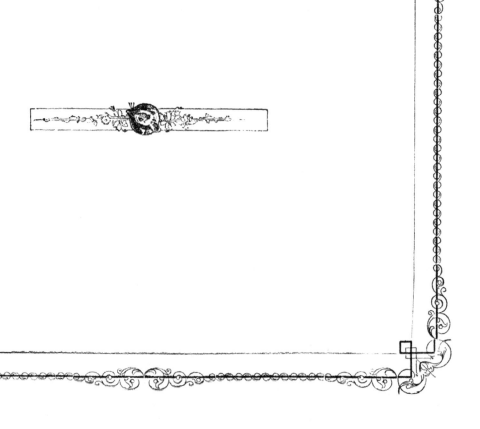

FABLE CXXVII.

THE HERON.

ONE day, on his stilt legs, walked, here and there,
    A Heron, with long neck and searching beak;
Along a river side he came to seek.
The water was transparent, the day fair,
    Gossip, the Carp, was gambolling in the stream
The Pike, her neighbor, was in spirits, too.
The Heron had no trouble, it would seem,
    But to approach the bank, and snap the two;
But he resolved for better appetite
    To calmly wait:—he had his stated hours:
He lived by rule. At last, there came in sight
    Some Tench, that exercised their finny powers
They pleased him not, and so he waited still,
Scornful, like rat of whom good Horace wrote.
"What! eat a tench?—I, who can take my fill,
Munch such poor trash?"—he'll sing another note.

THE HERON.

The Tench refused, a gudgeon next came by:
"A pretty dish for such as me, forsooth!
The gods forgive me if I eat such fry:
I'll never open beak for that:"—and yet, in truth,
He opened for far less.   The fish no more
Returned.   Then Hunger came;—thus ends my tale.
He who'd rejected dishes half a score,
Was forced, at last, to snap a paltry snail.

Do not be too exacting.   The cleverer people are
The sooner pleased, by far.
We all may lose by trying for too much;—
    I have known such.
Hold nothing in contempt, and the less so,
If you are needing help, for know
In that trap many fall, not only birds,
Like Herons, to whom now I gave some words.
Listen, my fellow-men,—another fable;
Some lessons can be found amid your lords.

FABLE CXXVIII.

THE MAN BADLY MARRIED.

OH, that the good and beautiful were wedded!
　　From early morrow I will seek the pair;
But since they are divorced, the addle-headed
　　Alone would track them long through sea or air.
Few beauteous bodies shelter beauteous souls;
　　So don't be angry if I cease pursuit.
Marriages many I have seen.　The goals
　　To which men strive my fancies seldom suit.

The full four-fourths of men rush reckless on,
　　And brave the deadliest risks;—four-fourths repent.
I'll produce one who being woe-begone,
　　Found no resource but sending where he'd sent
Before his hopeless wife, jealous and miserly,
　　Peevish and fretful;—nothing was done right.
They went to bed too soon—rose tardily;

THE MAN BADLY MARRIED

The white was black, the black was staring white;
The servants groaned, the master swore outright.
"Monsieur is always busy; he, of course,
Will think of nothing—squanders everything."
So much of this, in fact, Monsieur, *par force*,
Weary of all this squabble, and the sting,
Sends her back to the country and her friends,—
Phillis, who drives the turkeys, and the men
Who watch the pigs, and very soon she mends.
Grown calmer, he writes for her kindly then:—
"Well, how did time pass? was it pleasant there?
How did you like the country innocence?"
"It's bearable," she said; "the only care
That vexed me was to see the vile pretence
Of industry. Why, those base, lazy patches
Let the herds starve;—not one of them has sense
To do their proper work, except by snatches."
"Come, madam," cried the husband, in a rage,
"If you're so peevish that folk out all day
Weary of you, and long to see the stage
That bears you from them anywhere away,
What must the servants feel who, every hour,
Are chased about by your outrageous tongue!
And what the husband who is in your power
By night and day? Adieu! May I be hung
If I again recall you from the farm;
Or if I do, may I atone the sin
By having Pluto's gloomy realms within
Two wives like you, a shrew for either arm."

FABLE CXXIX.

THE MAIDEN.

A CERTAIN Maiden, somewhat proud,
　　A husband sought from out the crowd
Of suitors.　Handsome he's to be, and bold.
Agreeable, young, and neither cold
Nor jealous.　Wealth she wished, and birth,
Talent; in fact, all things on earth.
Who could expect to have them all?
Fortune was kind and helped to call
Lovers of rank and eminence.
She thought them mean and wanting sense—
"What! I accept such people?　Pish!
You're doting, if that is your wish.
Look at the paltry creatures.　See;
Mark how they grin, and ogle me."
One's vulgar; he who dares propose

THE MAIDEN.

THE MAIDEN.

Has, goodness gracious! such a nose;
This is too short, and that too tall,
Something distinctly wrong in all.
Affected girls are hard to please,
Though lovers sue them on their knees.
After the best were spurned, there came
The humbler people of less name.
She mocked them, too, unmercifully—
"To greet such men is good of me;
Perhaps they think my chance is poor,
Even to venture near my door;
But, Heaven be thanked, I pass my life,
Although alone, quite free from strife."
The Belle was with herself content;
But age came soon, the lovers went.
A year or two passed restlessly;
Then comes chagrin, and by-and-by
She feels that every hurrying day
Chases first smiles, then love away.
Soon wrinkles make her almost faint,
And try a thousand sorts of paint;
But all in vain, when past one's prime,
To shun that mighty robber, Time:
A ruined house you can replace,
But not the ruins of a face.
Her pride abates—her mirror cries,
"A husband get if you are wise;"
Her heart, too, echoes what is said—
E'en prudes are willing to be wed

LA FONTAINE'S FABLES.

A curious choice, at last, she made,
And not a grand one, I'm afraid;
Her choice was what most men called foolish:
A clumsy boor, ill-shaped and mulish.

FABLE CXXX.

THE WISHES.

IN the Mogul's dominions far away,
   Certain small spirits there are often found,
Who sweep the house and dig the garden ground,
And guard your equipage by night and day:
If you but touch their work, you spoil the whole.
One of these spirits near the Ganges, then,
Toiled at the garden of a citizen:
And with a silent skill worked heart and soul.
He loved his master and his mistress, too,
The garden most. The Zephyrs (Heaven knows),
Friends of the genii, as the story goes,
Perhaps assisted him, whate'er he'd do.
He toiled unceasingly to show his zeal,
Loaded his host with gifts, a brimming store,
Boundless of pleasure; indeed, wished no more
To leave those friends for whom he thus could feel.

Fickle such spirits are, yet true was he;
His brother genii, joining in a plot,
The chief of their republic quickly got,
From some caprice or jealous policy,
To order him to go to Norway straight,
To guard a hut covered with changeless snows,
From India straight to Lapland. Ere he goes
The Spirit with his master holds debate :
"They make me leave you, yet I know not why,
For some forgotten fault, and I obey;
But be the time a month, or but a day,
I'll grant you now Three Wishes ere I fly—
Three, and no more. It is not hard, I know,
For man to wish—how easy, we all see."
They wished Abundance, and then presently
Abundance came; fast from her full hands flow
The golden streams, barns brim with piles of wheat;
The cellars with rich casks are almost burst :
How to arrange the stores—that is the worst;
What ceaseless care! what toil of hands and feet!
Thieves plot against them; nobles will still borrow;
The Prince heaps taxes : hapless is their fate;
Their sorrow too much fortune, luck too great.
They say, "Take from us wealth, let's wake to-morrow
Poor as before. Happy the indigent;
Poverty's better than such wealth," their cry :
"Treasures, begone, take wings at once, and fly;
Of that so foolish wish we both repent.
Come, Moderation, mother of Repose,

THE WISHES.

Friend of good sense, O Moderation, come!"
She comes once more unto her former home;
The door behind her joyfully they close.
Two wishes gone, and not so luckily,
Their lot was that of those who dream away
Life in vain sighings, stealing, day by day,
Time better spent in honest industry.
The Spirit smiled at them; ere taking flight,
While yet his wings were spread, the one wish more
They asked; and this time Wisdom—that's a store
That never can embarrass, day or night.

FABLE CXXXI.

THE VULTURES AND THE PIGEONS.

MARS one day set the sky on fire:
    A quarrel roused the wild birds' ire—
Not those sweet subjects of the spring,
Who in the branches play and sing;
Not those whom Venus to her car
Harnesses; but the Vulture race,
With crooked beak and villain face.
'Twas for a dog deceased—that's all.
The blood in torrents 'gins to fall;
I only tell the sober truth,
They fought it out with nail and tooth.
I should want breath for the detail,
If I told how with tooth and nail
They battled. Many chiefs fell dead,
Many a dauntless hero bled;

THE VULTURES AND THE PIGEONS.

THE VULTURES AND THE PIGEONS.

Prometheus on his mountain sighed,
And hoped Jove nearly satisfied.
'Twas pleasure to observe their pains—
'Twas sad to see the corpse-strewn plains.
Valor, address, and stratagem,
By turns were tried by all of them;
By folks so brave no means were lost
To fill each spare place on the coast
Of Styx. Each varied element
Ghosts to the distant realm had sent.
This fury roused, at last, deep pity
Within the pigeons' quiet city;
They—of the neck of changing hue.
The heart so tender and so true—
Resolved, as well became their nation,
To end the war by mediation.
Ambassadors they chose and sent,
Who worked with such a good intent,
The Vultures cried, " A truce," at last,
And war's red horrors from them cast.
Alas! the Pigeons paid for it;
Their heart was better than their wit:
The cursed race upon them fell,
And made a carnage terrible;
Dispeopled every farm and town,
And struck the unwise people down.

In this, then, always be decided:
Keep wicked people still divided;

The safety of the world depends
On that—sow war among their friends;
Contract no peace with such, I say,
But this is merely by the way.

FABLE CXXXII.

THE COURT OF THE LION.

HIS Majesty Leo, in order to find
    The extent of his varied and ample dominions,
Had summoned his vassals of every kind,
Of all colors and shapes, and of divers opinions.
A circular, signed by His Majesty's hand,
Was the means of conveying the King's invitation—
He promised festivities regally grand
(With an evident eye to self-glorification).
His palace was open, of course, to the throng;
What a place!—a mere slaughter-house, putting it plainly,
Where visitors met with an odor so strong
That they strove to protect their olfactories vainly.
The Bear in disgust put a paw to his nose;
He had scarcely the time to repent his grimaces;
For Leo at once in a fury arose,
And consigned the poor brute to the Styx, to make faces.

The Monkey, true courtier, approved of the deed—
Said the palace was fit for a king's habitation,
And thought neither amber nor musk could exceed
The rich odor that gave him such gratification.
His fulsome behavior had little success;
He was treated the same as the previous aspirant
(His Leonine Majesty, let us confess,
Was Caligula-like, and a bit of a tyrant).
The Fox trotted up, very servile and sly;
Said the monarch, "No shuffling, but answer me frankly;
Beware how you venture to give your reply:
Do you notice that anything smells rather rankly?"
But Reynard was more than a match for his king,
And replied that his cold being rather a bad one,
He could not at present distinguish a thing
By its odor, or even assert that it *had* one.

There's a hint for plain speakers and flatterers here—
You should ne'er be too servile nor over-sincere;
And to answer sometimes in a round-about way
Is a dozen times better than plain yea or nay.

THE MILK-MAID AND THE MILK-PAIL.

FABLE CXXXIII.

THE MILK-MAID AND THE MILK-PAIL.

PERETTE, her Milk-pail balanced on her head,
    Tripped gaily and without hindrance down the road,
So slim and trim, and gay she nimbly sped.
For more agility, with such a load,
She'd donned her shortest kirtle and light shoes.
And as she went she counted up her gains—
Her future gains—with her twice one, twice twos.
How long division racked her little brains!
"First buy a hundred eggs, then triple broods;
With care like mine the money soon will grow;
No fox so clever in our neighbor's woods
But must leave me enough, as well I know,
To buy a pig; 'twill fatten very soon;
I buy him large, and for a good round sum
I sell him, mark you that some afternoon;
A cow and calf into our stable come;

LA FONTAINE'S FABLES.

Who'll prevent that? that's what I mean to say.
I see the calf skipping among the herd."
Then Perette skipped for joy. Alack-a-day!
Down came the milk, I give you my sworn word
Adieu cow, calf, pig, chicken, all the rest.
She left with tearful eye her fortune lost,
And ran to tell her husband, dreading lest
He'd beat her, when in anger tempest tossed.
The neighbors, doubling up with laughter,
Called her the Milk-pail ever after.

Who has not raised his tower in Spain,
And in a cloud-land longed to reign?
Picrocolles, Pyrrhus have so done,
Sages or fools, just like this one.
All dream by turns; the dream is sweet;
The world lies prostrate at our feet:
Our souls yield blindly to the vision,
Ours beauty, honor, fields Elysian.
'Tis I alone the bravest smite;
The dethroned Sophy owns my might;
They choose me king; in crowds I'm led;
Gold crowns come raining on my head.
A fly soon wakes me up once more,
And I am Big John, as before.

FABLE CXXXIV.

THE CURATE AND THE CORPSE.

A DEAD man, on his mournful way,
   To his last lodging went one day.
A Curè, bustling gaily, came
In due form, to inter the same.
Deceased was in a coach, with care
Packed snugly from the sun and air;
Clad in a robe, alas! ye proud,
Summer or winter, called a shroud;
To change it no one is allowed.
The pastor sat the dead beside,
Reciting, without grief or pride,
Lessons, responses, and those done,
The funeral psalms; yes, every one.
Good Mr. Dead-man, let them chant,
The salary is all they want.
The Curè Chouart shut the eyes

Of his dead man, lest he surprise
The priest who snatched from him a prize.
His looks they seemed to say, " My friend,
From you I'll have, before I end,
This much in silver, that in wax,"
And many another little tax;
That soon would bring our good divine
A small cask of the choicest wine,
His pretty niece a new silk gown,
And Paquette something from the town.
Just as his pleasant thoughts took flight,
There came a crash. . . Curè, good night!
The leaden coffin strikes his head.
Parishioner, lapped up in lead,
Politely you went first, you see,
Now comes the priest for company.

Such is our life, as in this tale:
See Curè Chouart counting on his fee,
Like the poor girl with the milk-pail.

FABLE CXXXV.

THE MAN WHO RUNS AFTER FORTUNE, AND THE MAN WHO WAITS FOR HER.

IS there a man beneath the sun,
    Who does not after Fortune run?
I would I were in some snug place,
And high enough to watch the race
Of the long, scuffling, struggling train
That hunt Dame Fortune all in vain.
The phantom flies from land to land,
They follow with an outstretched hand.
Now they have almost caught her. No;
She's vanished like the April bow.
Poor creatures! Pity them, I do:
Fools deserve pity—the whole crew,
By no means rage—"You see, we hope;
That cabbage-planter made a Pope.
Are we not quite as good?" they cry.

LA FONTAINE'S FABLES.

"Twenty times better," my reply.
"But what avails your mighty mind,
When Fortune is so densely blind?
Besides, what use the Papacy?
It is not worth the price, may be."
Rest, rest; a treasure that's so great
'Twas once for gods reserved by Fate;
How rarely fickle Fortune sends
Such gifts unto her trusting friends.
Seek not the goddess; stay at home;
Then like her sex she's sure to come.
Two friends there lived in the same place,
Who were by no means in bad case.
One sighed for Fortune night and day:
"Let's quit our sojourn here, I pray,"
He to the other said, "You know
Prophets in their own country go
Unhonored; let us seek elsewhere."
"Seek!" said the other; "I'll stay here.
I wish no better land or sky:
Content yourself, and I will try
To sleep the time out patiently."
The friend—ambitious, greedy soul!—
Set out to reach the wished-for goal;
And on the morrow sought a place
Where fortune ought to show her face,
And frequently—the Court, I mean;
So there he halts to view the scene;
Still seeking early, seeking late,

FORTUNE AND HER ATTENDANTS.

The hours propitious to Fate;
But yet, though seeking everywhere,
He only found regret and care.
"It's of no use," at last he cried;
"Queen Fortune elsewhere must abide:
And yet I see her, o'er and o'er,
Enter by this and that man's door:
And how, then, is it I can never
Meet her, though I seek her ever?"
These sort of people, I'm afraid,
Ambition find a losing trade.
Adieu, my lords; my lords, adieu;
Follow the shadow ruling you.
Fortune at Surat temples boasts;
Let's seek those distant Indian coasts,
Ye souls of bronze who e'er essayed
This voyage; nay, diamond arms arrayed
The man who first crossed the abyss.
Many a time our friend, I wis,
Thought of his village and his farm,
Fearing incessantly some harm
From pirates, tempests, rocks and sands,
All friends of death. In many lands
Man seeks his foeman, round and round,
Who soon enough at home is found.
In Tartary they tell the man
That Fortune's busy at Japan:
Then off he hurries, ne'er downcast
Seas weary of the man at last,

And all the profit that he gains
Is this one lesson for his pains:
Japan, no more than Tartary,
Brought good to him or wealthy fee.
At last he settles it was shame
To leave his home, and takes the blame.
Then he returns: the well-loved place
Makes tears of joy run down his face.
"Happy," he cries, "the man at ease,
Who lives at home himself to please;
Ruling his passions, by report
Knowing alone of sea or Court,
Or Fortune, of thy empire, Jade,
Which has by turns to all displayed
Titles and wealth, that lead us on
From rising to the setting sun;
And yet thy promises astray
Still lead us to our dying day.
Henceforth I will not budge again,
And shall do better, I see plain."
While he thus schemed, resolved, and planned,
And against Fortune clenched his hand,
He found her in the open air
At his friend's door, and sleeping there.

THE TWO FOWLS.

FABLE CXXXVI.

THE TWO FOWLS.

TWO Barn-door Fowls in peace spent all their life
    Until, at last, love, love lit up the strife :
War's flames burst out. O Love! that ruined Troy,
'Twas thou who, by fierce quarrel, banished joy,
And stained with blood and crime the Xanthus' tide!
Long, long the combat raged 'tween wrath and pride,
Until the rumor spread the whole town through,
And all the crested people came to view.
Many a well-plumed Helen was the prize
Of him who conquered; but the vanquished flies—
Skulks to the darkest and most hidden place,
And mourns his love with a dejected face.
His rival, proud of recent victory,
Exulting crows, and claims the sovereignty.
The conquered rival, big with rage, dilates,
Sharpens his beak, and Fortune invocates,

Clapping his wings, while, maddened by defeat,
The other skulks and plans a safe retreat.
The victor on the roof is perched, to crow;
A vulture sees the bragger far below.
Adieu! love, pride, and glory, all are vain
Beneath the vulture's beak;—so ends that reign.
The rival soon returns to make his court
To the fair dame, and victory to report;
As he had half-a-dozen other wives, to say the least,
You'll guess the chattering at his wedding feast.

Fortune always rejoices in such blows:
Insolent conquerors, beware of those.
Still mistrust Fate, and dread security,
Even the evening after victory.

FABLE CXXXVII.

THE COACH AND THE FLY.

UP a long, dusty hill, deep sunk in sand,
    Six sturdy horses drew a Coach. The band
Of passengers were pushing hard behind:
Women, old men, and monks, all of one mind.
Weary and spent they were, and faint with heat;
Straight on their heads the sunbeams fiercely beat.
In the hot air, just then, came buzzing by,
Thinking to rouse the team, a paltry Fly.
Stings one and then another; views the scene;
Believing that this ponderous machine
Is by his efforts moved, the pole bestrides;
And now upon the coachman's nose he rides.
Soon as the wheels begin again to grind
The upward road, and folks to push behind,
He claims the glory; bustles here and there,
Fussy and fast, with all the toil and care

With which a general hurries up his men,
To charge the broken enemy again,
The victory secure. The Fly, perplexed
With all the work, confessed that she was vexed.
No one was helping in that time of need.
The monk his foolish breviary would read :
He chose a pretty time ! a woman sang :
Let her and all her foolish songs go hang !
Dame Fly went buzzing restless in their ears,
And with such mockery their journey cheers.
After much toil, the Coach moves on at last :
" Now let us breathe ; the worst of it is past."
The Fly exclaimed : " it is quite smooth, you know ;
Come, my good nags, now pay me what you owe."

So, certain people give themselves great airs,
And meddlers mix themselves with one's affairs ;
Try to be useful, worry more and more,
Until, at last, you show the fools the door.

FABLE CXXXVIII.

THE INGRATITUDE AND INJUSTICE OF MEN TOWARDS FORTUNE.

A MERCHANT, trading o'er the seas,
    Became enriched by every trip.
No gulf nor rock destroyed his ease;
    He lost no goods from any ship.

To others came misfortunes sad,
    For Fate and Neptune had their will.
Fortune for him safe harbors had;
    His servants served with zeal and skill.

He sold tobacco, sugar, spices,
    Silks, porcelains, or what you please;
Made boundless wealth (this phrase suffices)
    And " lived to clutch the golden keys."

'Twas luxury that gave him millions:
   In gold men almost talked to him.
Dogs, horses, carriages, postillions,
   To give this man seemed Fortune's whim.

A Friend asked how came all this splendor:
   "I know the 'nick of time,'" he said,
"When to be borrower and lender:
   My care and talent all this made."

His profit seemed so very sweet,
   He risked once more his handsome gains;
But, this time, baffled was his fleet:
   Imprudent, he paid all the pains.

One rotten ship sank 'neath a storm,
   And one to watchful pirates fell;
A third, indeed, made port in form,
   But nothing wanted had to sell.

Fortune gives but one chance, we know;
   All was reversed,—his servants thieves.
Fate came upon him with one blow,
   And made the mark that seldom leaves.

The Friend perceived his painful case.
   "Fortune, alas!" the merchant cries.
"Be happy," says his Friend, "and face
   The world, and be a little wise.

MEN'S TREATMENT OF FORTUNE.

To counsel you is to give health:
  I know that all mankind impute
To Industry their peace and wealth,
  To Fortune all that does not suit."

Thus, if each time we errors make,
  That bring us up with sudden halt,
Nothing's more common than to take
  Our own for Fate or Fortune's fault.

Our good we always make by force,
  The evil fetters us so strong;
For we are always right, of course,
  And Destiny is always wrong.

FABLE CXXXIX.

AN ANIMAL IN THE MOON.

SOME sages argue that all men are dupes,
    And that their senses lead the fools in troops;
Other philosophers reverse this quite,
And prove that man is nearly always right.
Philosophy says true; senses mislead,
If we judge only by them without heed;
But if we mark the distance and reflect
On atmosphere and what it will effect,
The senses cheat none of us; Nature's wise:
I'll give an instance. With my naked eyes
I see the sun; how large is it, think you?
Three feet at farthest? It appears so, true!
But could I see it from a nearer sky,
'Twould seem of our vast universe the eye:
The distance shows its magnitude, you see;
My hand discovers angles easily.

AN ANIMAL IN THE MOON.

AN ANIMAL IN THE MOON.

Fools think the earth is flat; it's round, I know;
Some think it motionless, it moves so slow.
Thus, in a word, my eyes have wisdom got,
The illusions of the senses cheat me not.
My soul beneath appearances sees deep;
My eye's too quick, a watch on it I keep;
My ear, not slow to carry sounds, betrays;
When water seems to bend a stick ten ways,
My reason helps me out, and if my sight
Lies always, yet it never cheats me quite:
If I would trust my senses, very soon
They'd tell me of the woman in the moon.
What is there really?—No, mistrust your eyes,
For what you see are inequalities.
The surface of the moon has many regions;
Here spread the plains, there mountains rise in legions,
In light and shade strange figures you can trace—
An elephant, an ox, a human face.
Not long ago in England, men perplexed,
Saw, in a telescope, what *savants* vexed,
A monster in this planet's mirror fair;
Wild cries of horror filled the midnight air.
Some change was pending—some mysterious change,
Predicting wars, or a misfortune strange.
The monarch came, he favored learned men;
The wondrous monster showed itself again:
It was a mouse between the glasses shut—
The source of war—the nibbler of a nut.
The people laughed—oh, nation blessed with ease,

LA FONTAINE'S FABLES.

When will the French have time for toils like these?
Mars brings us glory's harvests; still the foe
Shrinks down before us, dreading every blow;
'Tis we who seek them, sure that victory,
Slave to our Louis, follows ceaselessly
His flag; his laurels render us renowned:
Yet memory has not left this mortal round.
We wish for peace—for peace alone we sigh;
Charles tastes the joys of rest; he would in war
Display his valor, and his flag bear far,
To reach the tranquil joy that now he shares.
Would he could end our quarrels and our cares!
What incense would be his, what endless fame!
Did not Augustus win a glorious name,
Equal to Cæsar's in its majesty,
And worthy of like reverence, may be?
Oh, happy people, when will Peace come down,
To dower our nation with her olive-crown?

FABLE CXL.

THE FORTUNE-TELLER.

OPINION is the child of Chance,
    And this Opinion forms our taste.
Against all people I advance
    These words. I find the world all haste—
Infatuation; justice gone;
    A torrent towards a goal unseen.
We only know things will be done
    In their own way, as they have been.

In Paris lived a Sorceress,
    Who told the people of their fate.
All sought her:—men; girls loverless;
    A husband whom his wife thought late
In dying; many a jealous woman.
    Ill-natured mothers, by the score,

Came—for they all were simply human—
    To hear what Fortune had in store.

Her tricks of trade were hardihood,
    Some terms of art, a neat address.
Sometimes a prophecy proved good,
    And then they thought her nothing less
Than Delphi's Pythoness of yore:
    Though ignorance itself was she:
And made her wretched garret floor
    Highway for gullibility.

Grown rich, she took a house, and bought
    A place of profit for her lord.
The witch's garret soon was sought
    By a young girl, who never soared
To witchery, save by eyes and voice.
    But yet they all came, as of old—
The lucky, who in wealth rejoice,
    And poor—to have their fortunes told.

The regulation had been made
    For this poor place, by her who late
Had been its tenant; and the shade
    Sybillic hovered o'er its state;
In vain the maiden said, "You mock.
    Read Fate!—I scarcely know my letters!"
But though such words, of course, might shock,
    They never could convince "her betters."

THE FORTUNE-TELLER.

THE FORTUNE-TELLER.

" Predict—divine;—here's gold in pay,
    More than the learned get together."
What wonder if the maid gave way,
    Despite herself, such gold to gather?
For fortune-telling seemed the place
    All tumble-down, and weird and broken:
A broomstick, for the witches' chase,
    And many another mystic token;

The witches' sabbath; all suggested
    The change of body, and of face;
And so in Fate fools still invested.
    But what of her who made the place?
She seeks the golden prize to gain,
    In gorgeous state like any parrot;
But people jeer and pass. In vain;
    They all go rushing to the garret.

'Tis custom governs everything.
    I've often seen, in courts of law,
Some stupid barrister, who'll bring
    Briefs such as clever men ne'er saw.
All a mistake: his eyes may glisten;
    They'll take him for some other man:
One unto whom the world will listen.
    Explain me this, now, if you can.

FABLE CXII.

THE COBBLER AND THE BANKER.

A COBBLER, who would sing from dawn to dark
    (A very merry soul to hear and see,
As satisfied as all the Seven Wise Men could be),
Had for a neighbor, not a paltry clerk,
But a great Banker, who could roll in gold :
A Crœsus, singing little, sleeping less ;
Who, if by chance he had the happiness,
Just towards morning, to drop off, I'm told,
Was by the Cobbler's merry singing woke.
Loud he complain'd that Heaven did not keep
For sale, in market-places, soothing sleep.
He sent, then, for the Cobbler ('twas no joke) :—
"What, Gregory, do you earn in the half-year?"
"Half-year, sir!" said the Cobbler, very gaily;
"I do not reckon so. I struggle daily
For the day's bread, and only hunger fear."

THE COBBLER AND THE BANKER.

THE COBBLER AND THE BANKER.

"Well, what a day:—what is your profit, man?"
"Now more, now less;—the worst thing is those fêtes.
Why, without them—and hang their constant dates!—
The living would be tidy—drat the plan!
Monsieur the Curé always a fresh saint
Stuffs in his sermon every other week."
The Banker laughed to hear the fellow speak,
And utter with such *naiveté* his complaint.
"I wish," he said, "to mount you on a throne;
Here are a hundred crowns, knave—keep them all:
They'll serve you well, whatever ill befall."
The Cobbler thought he saw before him thrown
All money in the earth that had been found.
Home went he to conceal it in a vault,
Safe from discovery and thieves' assault.
There, too, he buried joy,—deep under ground;
No singing now: he'd lost his voice from fear.
His guests were cares, suspicions, vain alarms;
All day he watch'd—at night still dreading harms:
If but a cat stirr'd, robbers he could hear.
At last the poor fool to his neighbor ran;
He had not woke him lately, I'm afraid:
"Return my songs and tranquil sleep," he said,
"And take your hundred crowns, my generous man."

FABLE CXLII.

THE CAT, THE WEASEL, AND THE LITTLE RABBIT.

A LITTLE Rabbit's charming nook
    A Weasel seized upon one morn;
His household gods with him he took,
    Jane Rabbit's mansion to adorn.

At break of day departed Jane,
    To munch amongst the thyme and roses,
Returning, at her window-pane—
    "Why, there the wicked Weasel's nose is!"

"Oh, gracious goodness! what is here?
    Turned out of my paternal hall!
From this you quickly disappear,
    Or I'll give all the rats a call."

The Weasel simply said the Earth
    Always belonged to the first comer;

THE CAT, THE WEASEL AND THE LITTLE RABBIT

All other claims were little worth:
    A sufferance tenant a misnomer.

A little kingdom he had found:
    "Now, tell me, what more right have you
To these domains, this patch of ground,
    Than Tom or Dick, than Nan or Sue?"

"Usage and custom of the law,"
    The Rabbit said, "give me the place:
On sire's and grandsire's claims I stand—
    I, who here represent their race."

"A law most wise! can't be more wise!"
    Said cunning Weasel. "What of that?
Our claims to settle, I devise
    A reference to our friend the Cat."

It was a Cat of solemn mien—
    A very hermit of a Cat:—
A saint, upon whose face was seen
    Precept and practice, law, and—fat.

The Rabbit here agreed, and then
    They sought the pious Pussy's home.
"Approach—I'm deaf," he said; and when
    They came, they told him why they'd come.

"Approach; fear not, for calm is law;
    For law no one here ever lacks;"

And, stretching on each side a claw,
    He broke both litigants' weak backs.

This story calls unto my mind
    The sad result which often springs
From squabbles of a larger kind,
    Which small grand-dukes refer to kings.

THE LION, THE WOLF, AND THE FOX.

FABLE CXLIII.

THE LION, THE WOLF, AND THE FOX.

A LION, sickly, weak, and full of years,
    Desired a remedy against old age
(*Impossible's* a word no monarch hears
    Without directly flying in a rage).
He sent for doctors—men of draughts and pills;
    From far and near, obedient to the call,
Came makers-up of recipes and pills;
    The Fox alone declined to come at all.
At court the Wolf malignantly referred
    To Reynard's absence, whereupon the King—
Whose anger was aroused at what he heard—
    Decided on a rather cruel thing,
And sent a force to smoke sly Reynard out,
    And bring him, willy nilly. When he came,
The Fox could scarcely entertain a doubt
    As to whose tongue had put him thus to shame.

"I greatly fear, your Majesty," said he,
    "You think me rude; you wrong me, if you do:
For I was on a pilgrimage, you see,
    And went to offer up my vows for *you*.
I scarcely need inform you I have met
    Expert physicians whilst I was away,
And hope to cure you of your sickness yet,
    Which comes from coldness of the blood, they say.
You must, sire, skin a Wolf, and wrap the skin
    About you close, to get the body warmed;
And when the heat has kindled up within
    The fires of life again, the cure's performed.
Our friend, I'm sure, will take immense delight
    In lending you his coat; so, take it, sire."
The Lion supped upon the Wolf that night,
    And made the skin a part of his attire.

Courtiers, discretion is your safest plan:
    Malice is sure to find its source again;
And, while you do yourself what good you can,
    Reflect that slandering others is in vain.

FABLE CXLIV.

THE HEAD AND THE TAIL OF THE SERPENT

THE Snake has two parts, it is said.
    Hostile to man—his tail and head;
And both, as all of us may know,
Are well known to the Fates below.
Once on a time a feud arose
For the precedence—almost blows.
" I always walked before the Tail,"
So said the Head, without avail.
The Tail replied, " I travel o'er
Furlongs and leagues—ay, score on score—
Just as I please. Then, is it right
I should be always in this plight?
Jove! I am sister and not slave:
Equality is all I crave.
Both of the selfsame blood, I claim
Our treatment, then, should be the same.

As well as her I poison bear,
Powerful and prompt, for men to fear.
And this is all I wish to ask;
Command it—'tis a simple task:
Let me but in my turn go first;
For her 'twill be no whit the worst.
I sure can guide, as well as she;
No subject for complaint shall be."
Heaven was cruel in consenting:
Such favors lead but to repenting.
Jove should be deaf to such wild prayers:
He was not then; so first she fares;
She, who in brightest day saw not,
No more than shut up in a pot,
Struck against rocks, and many a tree—
'Gainst passers-by, continually;
Until she led them both, you see,
Straight into Styx.   Unhappy all
Those wretched states who, like her, fall.

PREFACE.

THE indulgence with which some of my fables have been received* has induced me to hope that this present collection may meet with the same favor. At the same time I must admit that one of the masters of our eloquence † has disapproved of the plan of rendering these fables in verse, since he believes that their chief ornament consists in having none; and that, moreover, the restraints of poetry, added to the severity of our language, would frequently embarrass me, and deprive most of these narratives of that brevity, which may be styled the very soul of the art of story-telling, since without it a tale necessarily becomes tame and languid. This opinion could only have been expressed by a man of exquisite taste, and I will merely ask of him that he will in some degree relax it, and will admit that the Lacedemonian graces are not so entirely opposed to the French language, that it is impossible to make them accord.

After all, I have but followed the example, I will not say of the ancients, which would not affect me in this case, but that of the moderns. In every age, amongst every poetical people, Parnassus has deemed this species of composition its own. Æsop's fables had scarcely seen the light when Socrates ‡ thought proper to dress them in the livery of the Muses;

---

* Before the year 1668, when the present collection of fables was first published, Fontaine had already published a few separately, and others had circulated in manuscript.

† Patru, a celebrated lawyer, a member of the French Academy, and one of La Fontaine's friends, who made a strange mistake in trying to divert him from a species of composition which has immortalized him.

‡ These fables had long been known when Socrates came into the world, and the Father of Philosophy only took the trouble to render them into verse during the imprisonment which preceded his death.

PREFACE.

and what Plato says on this subject is so pleasant, that I cannot refrain from making it one of the ornaments of this Preface. He says, then, that Socrates, having been condemned to death, his punishment was respited on account of the occurrence of certain fetes. Cébès went to see him on the day of his death, and Socrates then told him that the gods had several times warned him by dreams that he should devote himself to music before he died. He did not at first understand the signification of these dreams: for, as music does not improve a man's moral nature, of what use could it be to him?* It was evident, however, that there was some mystery involved, for the gods never ceased to give him the same warning, and it had come to him again on the occasion of one of the fetes to which I have above alluded. At length, after having deeply reflected on what it might be that Heaven intended him to do, he concluded, that as music and poetry are so closely allied, it probably meant him to turn his attention to the latter. There can be no good poetry without harmony; but to good poetry fiction is also equally necessary, and Socrates only knew how to tell the truth. At length, however, he discovered a compromise; selecting such fables as those of Æsop, which always contain something of truth in them, he employed the last moments of his life in rendering them into verse.

Socrates is not the only one who has regarded fables and poetry as sisters. Phædrus has also declared that he held this opinion, and by the excellence of his work we are able to judge of that of the philosopher. After Phædrus, Avienus treated the same subject in the same way; finally the moderns have also followed their example, and we find instances of this, not only amongst foreign nations, but in our own. It is true, that when our own countrymen devoted their attention to this species of composition the French language was so different from what it now is, that we may regard them in this case as foreigners. This has not deterred me from my enterprise. On the contrary, I have flattered myself with the hope that, if I did not pursue this career with success, I should at least earn the credit of having opened the road.

It may possibly happen that my labors will induce others to continue the work; and, indeed, there is no reason why this species of composition should be exhausted until there shall remain no fresh fables to put in

---

* The word Μουσιχὴ implied amongst the Greeks all the arts to which the Muses devote themselves. It comprises the employments of the mind in opposition to γυμναστιχὴ, which means the exercises of the body. La Fontaine does not give Plato's meaning quite correctly. The philosopher, at the commencement of the "Phædo," makes Socrates say that, having been several times warned in dreams by the gods to study music, he had only regarded it as an encouragement to persevere in the pursuit of truth; but that, since his imprisonment, he had given another interpretation to those warnings, and had decided that he should better obey the wishes of the gods by making verses.

verse. I have selected the best; that is to say, those which seem to me to be so; but in addition to the fact that I may have erred in my selection, it will be by no means a difficult thing for others to give a different rendering even to those which I have selected; and if their renderings should be briefer than mine, they will doubtless be more approved. In any case, some praise will always be due to me, either because my rashness has had a happy result, and that I have not departed too far from the right path, or, at least, because I shall have instigated others to do better.

I think that I have sufficiently justified my design. As regards the execution, I shall leave the public to be the judge. There will not be found in my renderings the elegance and extreme brevity which are the charms of Phædrus, for these qualities are beyond my powers; and that being the case, I have thought it right to give more ornament to my work than he has done. I do not blame him for having restricted himself in length, for the Latin language enabled him to be brief; and, indeed, if we take the trouble to examine closely, we shall find in this author all the genuine characteristics and genius of Terence. The simplicity of these great men is magnificent; but, not possessing the powers of language of these authors, I cannot attain their heights. I have striven, therefore, to compensate in some degree for my failings in this respect, and I have done this with all the more boldness because Quintilian has said that one can never deviate too much in narrative. It is not necessary in this place to prove whether this be true or not; it is sufficient that Quintilian has made the statement.* I have also considered that as these fables are already known to all the world, I should have done nothing if I had not rendered them in some degree new, by clothing them with certain fresh characteristics. I have endeavored to meet the wants of the day, which are novelty and gaiety; and by gaiety I do not mean merely that which excites laughter, but a certain charm, an agreeable air, which may be given to every species of subject, even the most serious.

It is not, however, by the outward form which I have given it that the value of my work should be alone judged, but by the quality of the matter of which it is composed, and by its utility. For what is there that is worthy of praise in the productions of the mind which is not to be found in the apologue? There is something so grand in this species of composition, that many of the ancients have attributed the greater part of these fables to Socrates; selecting as their author that individual amongst mortals who was most directly in communication with the gods.

---

* The following is the passage in Quintilian to which the poet alludes:—"Ego vero narrationem, at si ullam partem orationis, omni qua potest gratia et venere exorundam." *Quint.*, "*Hist. Orat.*," lib. ix., cap iv.

PREFACE.

I am rather surprised that they have not maintained that these fables descended direct from heaven,* or that they have not attributed their guardianship to some one special deity, as they have done in the case of poetry and eloquence. And what I say is not altogether without foundation, since, if I may venture to speak of that which is most sacred in our eyes in the same breath with the errors of the ancients, we find that Truth has spoken to men in parables; and is the parable anything else than a fable? that is to say, a feigned example of some truth, which has by so much the more force and effect as it is the more common and familiar?

It is for these reasons that Plato, having banished Homer from his Republic, has given a very honorable place in it to Æsop. He maintains that infants suck in fables with their mothers' milk, and recommends nurses to teach them to them, since it is impossible that children should be accustomed at too early an age to the accents of wisdom and virtue. If we would not have to endure the pain of correcting our habits, we should take care to render them good whilst as yet they are neither good nor bad. And what better aids can we have in this work than fables? Tell a child that Crassus, when he waged war against the Parthians, entered their country without considering how he should be able to get out of it again, and that this was the cause of the destruction of himself and his whole army, and how great an effort will the infant have to make to remember the fact! But tell the same child that the fox and the he-goat descended to the bottom of a well for the purpose of quenching their thirst, and that the fox got out of it by making use of the shoulders and horns of his companion as a ladder, but that the goat remained there in consequence of not having had so much foresight, and that, consequently, we should always consider what is likely to be the result of what we do,— tell a child these two stories, I say, and which will make the most impression on his mind? Is it not certain that he will cling to the latter version as more conformable and less disproportioned than the other to the tenderness of his brain? It is useless for you to reply that the ideas of childhood are in themselves sufficiently infantine, without filling them with a heap of fresh trifles. These trifles, as you may please to call them, are only trifles in appearance; in reality they are full of solid sense. And as by the definition of the point, the line, the surface, and the the other well-known elements of form, we obtain a knowledge which enables us to measures not only the earth but the universe, in the same manner, by the aid of the

---

* La Fontaine has not ventured altogether to repair the oversight of the ancients, for he has left the origin of fables a doubtful point between heaven and earth, when he says, in a dedication to Madame de Montespan, "The fable is a gift which comes from the immortals; if it were the gift of man, he who gave it us would indeed deserve a temple."

truths involved in fables, we finally become enabled to form correct opinions of what is right and what is wrong, and to take a foremost place in the ranks of life.

The fables which are included in this collection are not merely moral, but are, to a certain extent, an encyclopædia of the qualities and characteristics of animals, and, consequently, of our own; since we men are, in fact, but a summary of all that is good and bad in the lower ranks of creatures. When Prometheus determined upon creating man, he took the dominant characteristic of each beast, and of these various characteristics composed the human species. It follows, therefore, that in these fables, in which beasts play so great a part, we may each of us find some feature which we may recognize as our own. The old may find in them a confirmation of their experiences, and the young may learn from them that which they ought to know. As the latter are but strangers in the world, they are as yet unacquainted with its inhabitants; they are even unacquainted with themselves. They ought not to be left in this ignorance, but should be instructed as to the qualities of the lion, the fox, and so forth, and as to the why and the wherefore a man is sometimes compared to the said lion and fox. To effect this instruction is the object of these fables.

I have already overstepped the ordinary limits of a Preface, but I have still a few remarks to make on the principles on which the present work has been constructed.

The fable proper is composed of two parts, of which one may be termed the body, and the other the soul. The body is the subject-matter of the fable, and the soul is the moral. Aristotle will admit none but animals into the domain of fabledom, and rigorously excludes from it both men and plants. This rule, however, cannot be strictly necessary, since neither Æsop, Phædrus, nor any of the fabulists* have observed it; but, on the other hand, a moral is to a fable an indispensable adjunct, and if I have in any instances omitted it, it is only in those cases in which it could not be gracefully introduced, or in which it was so obvious that the reader could deduce it for himself. The great rule in France is to value only that which pleases, and I have thought it no crime, therefore, to cancel ancient customs when they would not harmonize with modern ones. In Æsop's time the fable was first related as a simple story, and then supplemented by a moral which was distinct in itself. Next Phædrus came, who was so

---

* The word *fabulist* was invented by La Fontaine, and has no equivalent either in the Greek or Latin languages. La Motte only ventured to use it under cover of the authority of our poet; and the French Academy, having declined to admit it into the first edition of its Dictionary, which was published after La Fontaine's death, only did so when it had been sanctioned by usage and public admiration.

far from complying with this rule, that he sometimes transposed the moral from the end to the commencement. For my own part, I have never ailed to follow Æsop's rule, except when it was necessary to observe a no less important one laid down by Horace, to the effect that no writer should obstinately struggle against the natural bent of his mind or the capabilities of his subject. A man, he asserts, who wishes to succeed, will never pursue such a course, but will at once abandon a subject when he finds that he cannot mould it into a creditable shape:

> "Et quæ
> Desperat tractata intescere posse, relinquit." *

It only remains to speak of the life of Æsop, whose biography by Planudes is almost universally regarded as fabulous. It is supposed that this writer formed the design of attributing a character and adventures to his hero which should bear some resemblance to his fables. This criticism, at first glance, appeared to me sufficiently specious, but I have since found that it has no solid basis. It is partly founded on what took place between Xantus and Æsop, and the quantities of nonsense there contrasted. To which I reply, Who is the sage to whom such things have not happened? The whole of the life even of Socrates was not serious; and what confirms me in my favorable opinion is, that the character which Planudes gives to Æsop is similar to that which Plutarch gives him in his Banquet of the Seven Wise Men—that is, the character of a keen and all-observant man. It may be objected, I know, that the Banquet of the Seven Wise Men is in itself a fiction; and I admit that it is possible to be doubtful about everything. For my own part, I cannot well see why Plutarch should have desired to deceive posterity on this subject, when he has professed to be truthful on every other, and to give to each of his personages his real character. But, however this may be, I would ask, Shall I be less likely to be believed if I endorse another man's falsehoods than if I invented some of my own? I might certainly fabricate a tissue of conjectures, and entitle them the "Life of Æsop;" but whatever air of genuineness it might wear, no one could rely upon such a work, and, if he must put up with fiction, the reader would always prefer that of Planudes to mine.

* Hor., "Ars Poet.," v. 150.

CONTENTS.

	PAGE.
The Grasshopper and the Ant	6
The Raven and the Fox	8
The Frog that wished to make Herself as big as the Ox	10
The Two Mules	11
The Wolf and the Dog	13
The Heifer, the She-Goat, and the Lamb, in partnership with the Lion	15
The Wallet	16
The Swallow and the Little Birds	18
The Town Rat and the Country Rat	21
The Man and his Image	24
The Dragon with many Heads, and the Dragon with many Tails	26
The Wolf and the Lamb	28
The Robbers and the Ass	31
Death and the Woodcutter	33
Simonides rescued by the Gods	36
Death and the Unhappy Man	39
The Wolf turned Shepherd	41
The Child and the Schoolmaster	43

	PAGE.
The Pullet and the Pearl	45
The Drones and the Bees	46
The Oak and the Reed	50
Against those who are Hard to Please	52
The Council held by the Rats	55
The Wolf pleading against the Fox before the Ape	58
The Middle-aged Man and the two Widows	60
The Fox and the Stork	62
The Lion and the Gnat	64
The Ass laden with Sponges, and the Ass laden with Salt	68
The Lion and the Rat	71
The Dove and the Ant	73
The Astrologer who let himself fall into the Well	75
The Hare and the Frogs	78
The two Bulls and the Frogs	81
The Peacock complaining to Juno	83
The Bat and the two Weasels	86
The Bird wounded by an Arrow	88
The Miller, his Son, and the Ass	89
The Cock and the Fox	94
The Frogs who asked for a King	97
The Dog and her Companion	99
The Fox and the Grapes	102
The Eagle and the Beetle	103
The Raven who wished to imitate the Eagle	106

CONTENTS.

	PAGE.
The Wolves and the Sheep	109
The Cat changed into a Woman	111
Philomel and Progne	114
The Lion and the Ass	116
The Cat and the old Rat	118
A Will interpreted by Æsop	122
The Lion in Love	126
The Fox and the Goat	130
The Shepherd and the Sea	133
The Drunkard and his Wife	135
King Gaster and the Members	137
The Monkey and the Dolphin	140
The Eagle, the Wild Sow, and the Cat	143
The Miser who lost his Treasure	145
The Gout and the Spider	149
The Eye of the Master	152
The Wolf and the Stork	156
The Lion defeated by Man	158
The Swan and the Cook	159
The Wolf, the Goat and the Kid	161
The Wolf, the Mother, and the Child	163
The Lion grown Old	166
The Drowned Woman	167
The Weasel in the Granary	169
The Lark and her Little Ones with the Owner of a Field	171
The Fly and the Ant	176
The Gardener and his Master	179
The Woodman and Mercury	182
The Ass and the little Dog	187
Man and the Wooden Idol	189
The Jay Dressed in Peacock's Plumes	191
The little Fish and the Fisherman	192
Battle Between the Rats and Weasels	195
The Camel and the Drift-wood	198
The Frog and the Rat	200
The Old Woman and her Servants	203
The Animals sending a Tribute to Alexander	206
The Horse wishing to be revenged on the Stag	210
The Fox and the Bust	212
The Horse and the Wolf	214
The Saying of Socrates	216
The Old Man and his Children	218
The Oracle and the Impious Man	221
The Mountain in Labor	223
Fortune and the Little Child	224
The Earthen Pot and the Iron Pot	227
The Hare's Ears	229
The Fox with his Tail cut off	231
The Satyr and the Passer-by	233
The Doctors	236
The Laboring Man and his Children	237
The Hen with the Golden Eggs	239
The Ass that carried the Relics	240
The Serpent and the File	241
The Hare and the Partridge	243
The Stag and the Vine	246
The Lion going to War	247
The Ass in the Lion's Skin	249
The Eagle and the Owl	251
The Shepherd and the Lion	253
The Lion and the Hunter	255
Phœbus and Boreas	257
The Bear and the two Friends	260
Jupiter and the Farmer	262
The Stag viewing himself in the Stream	265
The Cockerel, the Cat, and the Little Rat	267
The Fox, the Monkey, and the other Animals	269

CONTENTS.

PAGE.

Title	Page
The Mule that boasted of his Family	271
The Old Man and the Ass	272
The Countryman and the Serpent	274
The Hare and the Tortoise	276
The Sick Lion and the Fox	279
The Ass and his Masters	281
The Sun and the Frogs	283
The Carter stuck in the Mud	286
The Dog and the Shadow	288
The Bird-catcher, the Hawk, and the Skylark	289
The Horse and the Ass	291
The Charlatan	292
The Young Widow	295
Discord	297
The Animals sick of the Plague	300
The Rat who retired from the World	303
The Heron	305
The Man Badly Married	307
The Maiden	309
The Wishes	313
The Vultures and the Pigeons	316
The Court of the Lion	320
The Milk-maid and the Milk-pail	323
The Curate and the Corpse	325
The Man who runs after Fortune, and the Man who waits for her	327
The Two Fowls	332
The Coach and the Fly	334
The Ingratitude and Injustice of Men towards Fortune	336
An Animal in the Moon	339
The Fortune-teller	343
The Cobbler and the Banker	347
The Cat, the Weasel, and the Little Rabbit	350
The Lion, the Wolf, and the Fox	354
The Head and the Tail of the Serpent	356

Continued in Volume 2

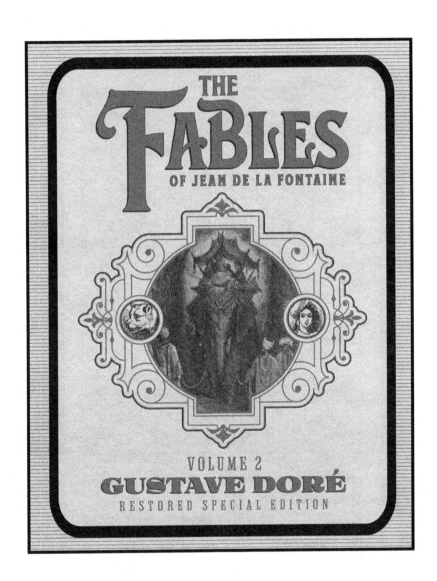

OTHER BOOKS FROM CGR PUBLISHING AT CGRPUBLISHING.COM

1939 New York World's Fair: The World of Tomorrow in Photographs

San Francisco 1915 World's Fair: The Panama-Pacific International Expo.

1904 St. Louis World's Fair: The Louisiana Purchase Exposition in Photographs

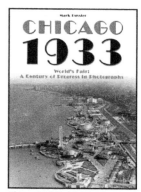
Chicago 1933 World's Fair: A Century of Progress in Photographs

19th Century New York: A Dramatic Collection of Images

The American Railway: The Trains, Railroads, and People Who Ran the Rails

The Aeroplane Speaks: Illustrated Historical Guide to Airplanes

The World's Fair of 1893 Ultra Massive Photographic Adventure Vol. 1

The World's Fair of 1893 Ultra Massive Photographic Adventure Vol. 2

The World's Fair of 1893 Ultra Massive Photographic Adventure Vol. 3

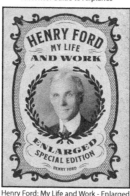
Henry Ford: My Life and Work - Enlarged Special Edition

Magnum Skywolf #1

Ethel the Cyborg Ninja Book 1

The Complete Ford Model T Guide: Enlarged Illustrated Special Edition

How To Draw Digital by Mark Bussler

Best of Gustave Doré Volume 1: Illustrations from History's Most Versatile...

OTHER BOOKS FROM CGR PUBLISHING AT CGRPUBLISHING.COM

Ultra Massive Video Game Console Guide Volume 1

Ultra Massive Video Game Console Guide Volume 2

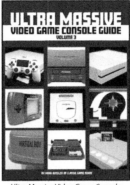
Ultra Massive Video Game Console Guide Volume 3

Ultra Massive Sega Genesis Guide

Antique Cars and Motor Vehicles: Illustrated Guide to Operation...

Chicago's White City Cookbook

The Clock Book: A Detailed Illustrated Collection of Classic Clocks

The Complete Book of Birds: Illustrated Enlarged Special Edition

1901 Buffalo World's Fair: The Pan-American Exposition in Photographs

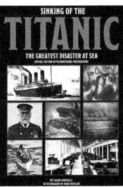
Sinking of the Titanic: The Greatest Disaster at Sea

Gustave Doré's London: A Pilgrimage: Retro Restored Special Edition

Milton's Paradise Lost: Gustave Doré Retro Restored Edition

The Art of World War 1

The Kaiser's Memoirs: Illustrated Enlarged Special Edition

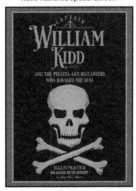
Captain William Kidd and the Pirates and Buccaneers Who Ravaged the Seas

The Complete Butterfly Book: Enlarged Illustrated Special Edition

- MAILING LIST -
JOIN FOR EXCLUSIVE OFFERS

www.CGRpublishing.com/subscribe

Made in the USA
Las Vegas, NV
11 September 2021